Exploring physics
Book One
SI EDITION

This is the first of five books, each covering a year's work in the secondary school. The author is senior lecturer in education at the University of Liverpool, and was formerly senior physics master at King George V School, Southport. His previous books, both published by John Murray, are *Electronics and Nuclear Physics* and *Practical Modern Physics*

Illustrated by **James K Hodgson**

John Murray

Tom Duncan

Exploring physics

Book One

SI EDITION

CONTENTS

© Tom Duncan 1968, 1970

First published 1968
Second edition (SI units) 1970
Reprinted 1971

Printed in Great Britain by Jarrold and Sons Ltd, Norwich

0 7195 2042 8

PREFACE

The present emphasis in science teaching is on pupils discovering by investigation, and on understanding rather than on the memorization of facts. This book has been written with these two points very much in mind. It is hoped that it will be helpful where the new approach is in use and teachers wish their pupils to have some background reading material showing the relevance of physics to everyday life and a fuller record of the course than their own notebooks provide: if more time is spent experimenting less is available for making notes.

An attempt has been made to produce a text offering:

(*a*) *A modern approach* in which the idea of atoms and molecules is introduced at an early stage and used subsequently to deal with a wide variety of topics.

(*b*) *Integrated theory and practical work* in which experiments play an important role in the development of a topic.

(*c*) *Questions* at appropriate points in the text requiring a certain amount of thought from the pupil, discussion in class or looking up.

(*d*) *Illustrative material* in the form of diagrams and plates to show physics in action in the world.

Many experiments and demonstrations are suggested. The former are intended to be performed by the class and the latter by the teacher, but this will depend on individual teachers and circumstances. The appendixes contain information about certain items of equipment.

The contents, the order of presentation of the topics and most of the practical work is very similar to that suggested for the first year of the Nuffield 'O' level physics scheme. I should therefore like to acknowledge my considerable debt to the organizers of this stimulating and challenging piece of curriculum development which promises to make a major contribution to science education in schools. I am also indebted to my friend and former colleague, Mr C. F. Flemming of King George V School, Southport, for his kindness in reading the manuscript and for the valuable comments he made. Finally, thanks are due to the artist for his excellent work and to my wife and daughters for their interest and assistance.

January 1968   T.D.

Second edition

This revised edition uses SI units.

Acknowledgments

Thanks are due to the following who have kindly permitted the reproduction of copyright photographs.

Page 1, B.A.C.; Fig. 1.3*a*, Aerofilms; 1.3*b*, Amalgamated Roadstone Corporation; 1.4*a,b*, National Coal Board; 1.5, Trustees of the British Museum (Natural History); 1.7, Geological Survey Office—Crown Copyright; 1.8 (*left*), Trustees of the British Museum (Natural History); 1.9, British Oxygen; 1.12, Radio Times Hulton Picture Library; 1.13, Cenco; 1.14, Professor Erwin Müller; page 13, J. Allan Cash; 2.1, Science Museum; 2.3, Radio Times Hulton Picture Library; 2.14, M. Byrne; 2.16, Courtaulds; 2.19, 2.20, I.C.I. Fibres; 2.22, I.C.I. Plastics; page 25, B.A.C.; 3.1, Dunlop Rubber Co.; 3.2, Burndept Ltd; 3.3, Associated Press; 3.7, W. F. Stanley and Co. Ltd; 3.8, Radio Times Hulton Picture Library; 3.22, National Physical Laboratory; page 39, Shell; 4.10, Paul Popper; 4.11*a,b*, W.A.S.A.-foto; 4.12, Science Museum; page 51, Fox Photos; 5.5, BBC Educational Publications; 5.9, Fox Photos; 5.10, Eidenbenz and Eglin, used in *Science*, ed. Bronowski (Aldus Books); page 61, I.C.I. Plastics; 6.5*a*, J. Allan Cash; 6.5*b*, Fox Photos; 6.12, French Tourist Office; 6.16, Science Museum; 6.35, British Travel Association; 6.36, Fox Photos; 6.39, U.S.I.S.; page 83, Science Museum; 7.15*a*, L. H. Newman (photo by W. J. C. Murray); 7.15*b*, Fox Photos; 7.15*c*, Focal Press (photo by Oskar Kreisel from *Focal Encyclopedia of Photography*); page 97, Sport and General; 8.4, *Muck Shifter*; 8.8, Rio Tinto; 8.9, 8.10, 8.11, U.K.A.E.A.; 8.12, Press Association; 8.15, A.E.R.E., Harwell.

Concorde supersonic airliner.
Developed and built jointly by
the British Aircraft Corporation
and Sud Aviation of France,
it is designed to cruise at
2300 km/h (1450 m.p.h.)

1 Matter

The variety of matter

An almost bewildering variety of materials exists on the earth. Rocks, soil, sea, air as well as living plants, animals and human beings, all occur naturally. Many other materials have been manufactured.

The scientific name for material is *matter*. One piece of matter can differ from another in size, shape, colour, feel, hardness, weight, smell, etc. These are called properties of matter.

Exhibition

Examine a wide range of common materials and try to put into groups or classes those that are alike in some ways.[1] A lever-arm balance (also called a Butchart balance) and a magnifying glass are available, Fig. 1.1. When using the magnifying glass hold it near to your eye and then move close to the object to be magnified until it is seen clearly.

[1] A list of suitable materials is given in Appendix 1, p. 108.

Fig. 1.1

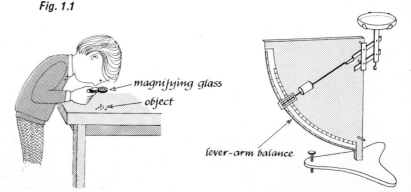

magnifying glass

object

lever-arm balance

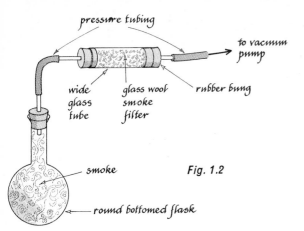

pressure tubing

to vacuum pump

wide glass tube

glass wool smoke filter

rubber bung

smoke

Fig. 1.2

round bottomed flask

removes the smoke (and therefore the air) *slowly*. If a rotary vacuum pump is used see Appendix 2, p. 108, for operating instructions and also keep the gas ballast valve open during the pumping, if there is one.

Q. 1.1 (*a*) How would you test that the label on a bottle marked 'vacuum' is correct?

(*b*) What similarities and differences are there between aluminium and lead?

When all the matter has been removed from a space we say that we have made a *vacuum*. An 'empty' bottle is usually full of air but most of it can be removed using a vacuum pump.

Demonstration 1.1. Action of a vacuum pump

Fill a round-bottomed flask with smoke from a piece of smouldering rope and then connect the flask and a glass-wool smoke trap to a vacuum pump, Fig. 1.2. Operate the pump so that it

Raw materials

The earth is a rich storehouse of materials. Some of these materials are used in their natural state whilst others, if properly treated, provide a whole host of products.

1. BUILDING INDUSTRY

Building materials are obtained directly from rocks such as marble, granite, slate, sandstone, flint and limestone. Fig. 1.3a shows a row of fifteenth-century Cotswold cottages built of local stone. Other essential items in the building industry are derived by processing materials

Fig. 1.3a

Fig. 1.3b

Fig. 1.4a

Fig. 1.4b

found on the earth. For example, bricks are made from clay, glass from sand, whilst cement, mortar and concrete are all obtained from limestone. Fig. 1.3b shows an excavator at work in a limestone quarry.

2. CHEMICAL INDUSTRY

Two important raw materials for the chemical industry are coal and crude oil. Nowadays most coal is cut by machines and removed from the coal face on conveyor-belts as shown in Figs. 1.4a and b. Apart from being burnt as a fuel in our homes, coal can be broken down to form thousands of materials. This is done by heating it to a high temperature in a container in which there is no air so that it cannot burn. Three by-products are formed—coal-gas, coke and coal-tar. The coal-gas can be used for heating and cooking, although in the not too distant future most of our domestic and industrial gas

supply will be natural gas (methane) obtained from under the North Sea. Coke is used as a fuel and to make steel. Coal-tar is the most remarkable of the three: nylon, detergents, perfumes, explosives, plastics, aspirin, saccharine, dyes, antiseptics and many other substances are all derived from it. Crude oil or petroleum is the thick, dark liquid obtained from underground deposits at oil-wells. It provides chemicals for the plastics industry as well as petrol, paraffin, oil and grease.

Scientists believe that coal was formed millions of years ago, when large areas of dense forest land settled below sea-level and were covered by mud and rocks. The trees had no chance to rot in the air but were squeezed so much that they changed into something very different—coal. Crude oil is thought to have been formed from the bodies of tiny animals and plants which were buried long ago.

4

Three-quarters of the earth's surface is covered by water to an average depth of about 4 kilometres (2½ miles). In the future the oceans may supply us with more and more food, raw materials and even fuel.

Fig. 1.5

Q. 1.2 What evidence is there to support the above explanation of how coal was formed? Does the piece of coal shown in Fig. 1.5 give you a clue?

The earth and its rocks

So far man has been able to penetrate only a short way into the earth but it is thought that it consists of a hard outer *crust*, up to 50 kilometres (30 miles) thick in places, which encloses a hot *core*, partly solid, partly liquid.

There are several theories about how the earth was formed but it seems likely that at the start it was very hot. As it cooled, rocks formed, granite probably being the first to appear on its surface, and the continents grew. Most of what we know about the history of the earth is the result of the study of the rocks by geologists.

Rocks are of three main types.

1. Igneous rocks such as granite were formed, as explained above, when the molten material in the earth's surface solidified.

2. Sedimentary rocks are the result of the crumbling action of wind and rain on igneous rocks over millions of years. The soil produced is carried by rivers to the sea-bed where the lower layers of the sediment so formed are pressed tightly together and, in time, harden into solid rock, Fig. 1.6. Layers of different kinds of sedimentary rock may form on top of each other and

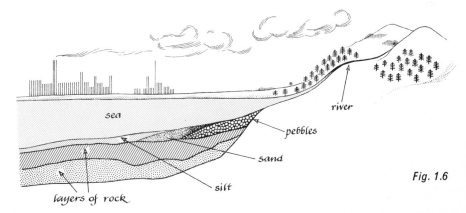

sea

river

pebbles

sand

silt

layers of rock

Fig. 1.6

Fig. 1.7

disturbances inside the earth may cause the layers to bend and sometimes to rise above sea-level. Can you see the folds in the layers of rock in Fig. 1.7? Limestone and sandstone are sedimentary rocks.

3. Metamorphic rocks are formed from either igneous or sedimentary rock when they are subjected to very high temperatures and pressures inside the earth. Marble has been formed from limestone in this way.

Q. 1.3 To which type of rock does each of the following belong: (*a*) clay, (*b*) slate, (*c*) coal?

Metals

Modern civilization could not exist without metals. In Roman times seven metals were known: iron, lead, tin, copper, silver, mercury and gold. Today we can produce over eighty.

Metals are rarely found in a pure state as gold sometimes is. They mostly occur in earthy-looking *ores*, joined with other substances from which they have to be separated. Separation can be achieved by heating the ore, usually very strongly. This process is called smelting. Whilst some ores lie just below the earth's surface, others are buried much deeper; in South Africa there are gold-mines about 3 kilometres (almost 2 miles) deep. Fig. 1.8 shows an ore of tin, and also some items used in physics, each of which contains one of the seven metals mentioned above.

Alloys are often more useful than pure metals. These are made by melting two or more metals so that they mix thoroughly together. Well-known alloys are bronze (copper and tin), brass (copper and zinc) and steel (iron and carbon). In Britain 'silver' coins do not contain silver but are made from an alloy of copper and nickel. In the

Fig. 1.8

1 Fuse wire (tin)   2 Battery (lead plates)
3 Electroscope (gold leaf)   4 Magnet (iron)
5 Reel of connecting wire (copper)   6 Mirror
(silver)   7 Thermometer (mercury)

aircraft industry aluminium alloy is used because it combines lightness and strength, even at high temperatures. A modern supersonic aircraft such as the Concorde, p. 1, is subjected to temperatures above that of boiling water when cruising at 2300 km/h (1450 m.p.h.).

Metals and alloys are very adaptable materials and can be made into sheets, tubes, wires, rods, etc. The ways in which each one is used depend on its particular properties.

Q. 1.4 Can you suggest why (*a*) steel girders are used in building construction; (*b*) saucepans are made of aluminium; (*c*) a galvanized dustbin is made from steel covered by a thin layer of zinc; and (*d*) 'tin' cans are made of steel sheet coated with tin?

Solid, liquid, gas

All matter can be divided into three groups known as the solid, the liquid and the gaseous (or vapour) states. Rock is a solid, water a liquid and air a gas. However, under suitable conditions each can change from one state to another. Thus, in a volcano rocks melt and become liquid and in very cold weather ponds freeze over, because when water is cooled it turns to ice, its solid form. You may have noticed on the roads, tankers like the one shown in Fig. 1.9 which carry air, oxygen or some other gas that has been liquefied by cooling to a very low temperature. A shooting star passes through all three states before it disappears. Therefore, although substances are most familiar in one particular state, they can change their state.

Fig. 1.9

Ice, water and steam are three states of the same substance. When ice melts it becomes water and when water is boiled it changes to steam. The changes from solid to liquid and from liquid to gas are brought about by heating. The reverse process of condensation (in which a gas becomes a liquid) and freezing (in which a liquid becomes a solid) occur by cooling.

Steam, like most gases and vapours, is invisible. If you look carefully at a kettle of boiling water you will see a gap between the end of the spout and the white cloud which is usually thought to be steam, Fig. 1.10. The steam is actually present in the gap and the white cloud consists of tiny drops of condensed steam, i.e. water.

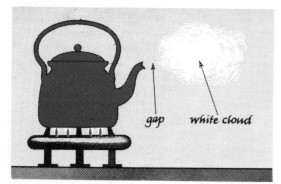

gap   white cloud

Fig. 1.10

Usually there is no difficulty in deciding the state of a substance, but doubtful cases do occur. Non-drip paint is one example. Another is the amusing substance called bouncing putty.[1] As well as flowing very slowly, it moulds like clay, stretches, can be shattered by a hammer blow

[1] Sold as 'potty putty' by Frido Ltd, Houldsworth Street, Reddish, Stockport, Cheshire.

and, when rolled into a ball, bounces. If the ball is left on a table it gradually collapses into a puddle of putty.

Q. 1.5 How do we decide whether something is a solid, a liquid or a gas? Why are liquids and gases sometimes called fluids?

Q. 1.6 Name substances like bouncing putty that are solid liquids.

Q. 1.7 Complete the following sentence: 'Changes of state occur when substances are . . . . . . or . . . .'

Elements

There are so many kinds of matter that any attempt to sort them out and make sense of them would seem doomed to failure. However, the position is not so complicated as appears at first sight. We now know as a result of a great deal of investigation that there are ninety-two basic substances, called *elements*, which cannot be broken down or decomposed into simpler substances. All other substances consist of two or more elements in combination and are called *compounds*. Water is a compound of the elements hydrogen and oxygen.

Iron, aluminium, gold, radium, mercury and silver are all elements. The lightest element is hydrogen which makes up about half of coal-gas; when liquefied hydrogen is used to fuel rockets. The heaviest element, uranium, is used as a fuel in nuclear power stations. Only a few of the ninety-two elements occur in nature on their own; most are combined with other elements. For example, iron is dug out of the ground as iron ore and this is a compound of iron and oxygen.

Our bodies contain over thirty elements with oxygen, carbon, hydrogen and nitrogen making up most of our weight. It is interesting to note that the colour of our hair probably depends on

A microscope really consists of two small magnifying glasses (lenses), one at each end of a short metal tube. The various parts are shown in Fig. 1.11. Some instruments have more than one

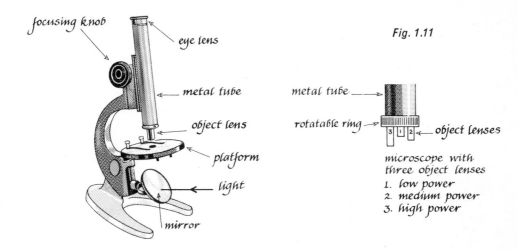

focusing knob

eye lens

metal tube

object lens

platform

light

mirror

Fig. 1.11

metal tube

rotatable ring

object lenses

microscope with
three object lenses
1. low power
2. medium power
3. high power

small amounts of certain metals. Fair hair contains titanium, red hair is due to molybdenum, brown hair is rich in copper, cobalt and iron, and grey hair has a larger proportion of nickel.

Very small amounts of about a dozen elements, all heavier than uranium, have been manufactured by nuclear scientists so that altogether there are just over one hundred.

The microscope

The microscope is one of the scientist's most useful tools for studying matter. It makes objects look larger so that details, otherwise invisible to the eye, are revealed.

object lens, each giving a different magnification when it is rotated into position above the hole in the platform. The object to be viewed is placed on a glass slide on the platform and the mirror tilted so that it reflects on to the object the maximum amount of light from a lamp placed near by on the bench. If more than one object lens is available the one of lowest power should be used first.

To view an object a convenient procedure is to turn the focusing knob until the object lens and the object are as close as possible. The knob is then turned in the *opposite direction* so that either the microscope tube moves up or, as in some instruments, the platform descends, until the magnified object is clearly seen.

Experiment 1.2. Viewing things with a microscope

Look at the following things always adjusting the microscope *carefully* in the way just explained:

    (*a*) a hair from your head
    (*b*) a piece of white paper or blotting paper
    (*c*) pencil or ink writing
    (*d*) any other object.

Write a few words in your notebook saying what you saw in each case.

    Girls may also like to examine threads of cotton, wool, silk, etc.

    We each have our own finger-print, a fact the police sometimes use! Press your thumb on an office ink-pad and then make a print on a piece of paper. Look at it first with an ordinary magnifying glass and then through the microscope. Compare what you see. Decide which of the four finger-prints shown in Fig. 1.12 yours is most like.

Atoms

If a piece of thin aluminium foil, usually but wrongly called 'silver paper', is cut into smaller and smaller pieces there comes a time when the piece is too small to hold. However, if it could be held, scientists *believe* that eventually cutting would produce a very tiny piece of aluminium that could not be cut and which would be too small to be seen even with the most powerful microscope. This tiniest piece of matter is called

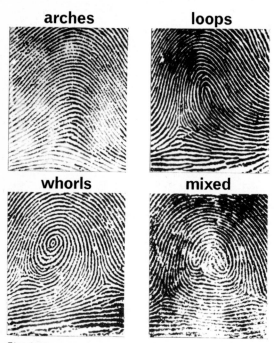

arches   **loops**

whorls   **mixed**

Fig. 1.12

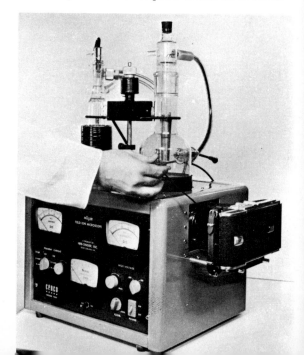

Fig. 1.13

Fig. 1.14

an *atom*. It is not unreasonable to assume that every one of the hundred or so elements has its own atoms, which are different from the atoms of every other element. The atoms of aluminium are not the same as the atoms of, say, copper.

Do atoms really exist? Is there any evidence to support our belief in them? If they do exist how small are they? A metal surface looks perfectly smooth and solid and shows no signs of being made up of particles, but so does a sandy beach when seen from a distance. If matter consists of atoms it could be that our eyes are just not good enough to see them directly and that some kind of 'scientific eye' is required.

Such an eye, known as the *field ion microscope*, Fig. 1.13, was invented in 1955 by Professor Erwin Müller. His instrument has a television-type screen on which pictures are produced, like the one in Fig. 1.14 of the tip of a metal needle viewed looking towards the point. Each dot of light *represents* an atom in the needle and the atoms are 'seen' in the same sense as we see things when we look at television.

There is other, indirect evidence for the existence of atoms which requires much less advanced apparatus than a field ion microscope and which we can obtain in a school physics laboratory, as we shall see later.

Although atoms were first suggested by the Greeks over 2000 years ago, it is only in the twentieth century that all scientists have become convinced of their existence.

Scientists and detectives

Scientists are continually faced with situations in which they have to investigate 'things' they cannot see or handle directly. It is as if the 'thing' was a locked 'black-box'. Ways have therefore to be devised of trying to make the 'thing' reveal its properties. Experiments are carried out involving certain actions, the results are carefully observed and conclusions drawn, but with caution. The scientist is rather like a detective. He has to seek clues patiently and then use his imagination and reasoning powers to piece the evidence together. Here is a piece of scientific detection work.

Experiment 1.3. Investigating 'black-boxes'[1]

The 'black-boxes' are coffee-tins, sealed with tape and each containing one 'thing'. The tins must not be opened but otherwise you can do anything you wish to discover the properties of the 'thing'. Try to form some idea of its size, its shape and perhaps the kind of material from which it is made.

[1] See Appendix 3, p. 109.

Giant's Causeway, Northern Ireland, where molten rock must have solidified during the cooling of the earth at its formation. In spite of weathering, the six-sided (hexagonal) shape of the rocks is clearly visible

2 Crystals

Crystals all around

Crystals are generally considered to be bits of matter that sparkle like diamonds and have hard, smooth faces with sharp edges.

Experiment 2.1. Crystal gazing

Look at large crystals of calcite and alum. Pick up separately crystals of preserving sugar, photographic hypo and common salt and examine them carefully with a magnifying glass.

You should now be able to say if all the crystals of a particular substance have (a) the same size and (b) the same shape. Make sketches in your notebook if you wish.

Experiment 2.2. Examining sugars with a microscope

Place a little granulated sugar on a glass slide and examine it, suitably illuminated, under a microscope. Is it crystalline? If it is, do the crystals have the same shape as those of preserving sugar?

Repeat with other sugars such as castor sugar, icing sugar, and answer the two previous questions in each case. If you cannot see crystals with a particular sugar can it be assumed that it is not crystalline? Give a reason for your answer.

Are crystals natural or man-made? Page 13 shows a photograph of the Giant's Causeway in Northern Ireland where molten rock must have solidified in crystals during the cooling of the earth at its formation. In spite of weathering their six-sided (hexagonal) crystalline shape is clearly visible. Fig. 2.1 shows quartz crystals of various sizes. Their shape is shown in Fig. 2.2. Quartz is one of the three crystalline substances that make up granite.

When water vapour in the air freezes, ice crystals are formed like those in Fig. 2.3. The shapes in this case are all different but

Fig. 2.1

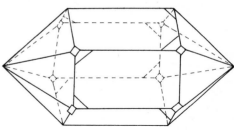

Fig. 2.2

every crystal is built on the same plan. Snow consists of millions of tiny ice crystals and so it is no wonder that newly fallen snow glistens brilliantly in sunshine.

Crystals are really much more common than appears at first sight and scientists believe that almost all solids are crystalline. In most cases, however, the solid consists of thousands of very small crystals joined together anyhow. With suitable preparation the crystalline form of many metals can be seen. Fan-like groups of zinc crystals are visible on the galvanized iron garden barrow in Fig. 2.4. If a piece of cast bismuth is available, you may be able to see the crystalline structure of its surface using a magnifying glass.

In fact, crystals are made by nature and each substance seems, in general, to prefer a particular shape. Very often, however, the same shape is used by crystals of different substances.

Q. 2.1 Can you spot from Fig. 2.3 the plan on which ice crystals are built?

Fig. 2.3

Fig. 2.4

Watching crystals grow

Perhaps the best proof that crystals are natural is obtained when they are seen growing.

Experiment 2.3. Watching hypo crystals grow

Fill one-third of a hard glass test-tube with photographic hypo crystals and heat them gently. The crystals lose their crystalline form by giving up water (called water of crystallization) in which they dissolve. Cool the liquid by letting cold water from a tap play against the side of the test-tube for a minute.

Hold the test-tube in your hand and drop one crystal of hypo into the cold liquid. What do you *see* happening? Do you *feel* anything happening? The experiment can be repeated by melting and cooling the hypo again.

The hypo crystal you drop in is called a 'seed' crystal. Why? What do you think would happen if you dropped in a sugar crystal instead of a hypo crystal? Try it.

Experiment 2.4. Watching salt crystals grow under a microscope

Fill one-third of a test-tube with water, add a little common salt and shake. If all the salt dissolves after a minute, add more until after shaking no more dissolves. You now have a *saturated solution* of salt in water.

Warm a microscope slide above a small Bunsen flame and place a drop of the salt solution on it. Focus a microscope on the edge of the drop and observe it until the solution has evaporated to dryness. Do your findings about the shape of salt crystals agree with those obtained in Experiment 2.1 when you examined them with a magnifying glass?

Crystal models and atoms

Why does a crystal have a regular shape which is generally the same for a particular substance? Is it due to the regular arrangement of the building bricks, possibly particles such as atoms, inside the crystal? Do crystals in fact offer some evidence for the existence of atoms?

Experiment 2.5. Making shapes with 'particles'

The 'particles' can be represented by fruit gums, Polo mints or simply by circles drawn round the unsharpened end of a round pencil on a piece of paper. Fig. 2.5 shows how such particles can

Fig. 2.5

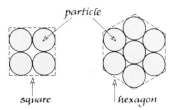

make four-sided (square) and six-sided (hexagonal) shapes. Try to make some other arrangements.

Can you make each of the shapes 'grow' so that they are larger but still of the same shape?

Demonstration 2.6. Large crystal models

A Expanded polystyrene balls, of 4 cm diameter, make good particles and can be glued together to show various three-dimensional crystal models as in Fig. 2.6.[1]

[1] Glue can be made by dissolving expanded polystyrene in amyl acetate (or acetone) until a syrupy liquid is obtained.

Fig. 2.6

Fig. 2.7

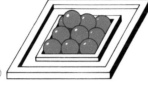
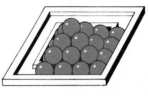

(a) baseboard (b) pyramid with 9 ball base (c) pyramid with 16 ball base

B A model of a growing crystal may be made using polystyrene balls and the special baseboard shown in Fig. 2.7a. A pyramid with a 9-ball base is first formed, Fig. 2.7b, and then more are added to give a pyramid with a 16-ball base, Fig. 2.7c, and a larger crystal. Finally a crystal with a 25-ball base can be 'grown' and compared with a large alum crystal.

Our models show that different shapes and sizes can be constructed from particles and they certainly do nothing to contradict the view that crystals owe their properties to being built in this way. Perhaps the most striking clue about atoms from crystals is given when they split.

Cleaving crystals

There are certain directions in which a crystal most easily splits or cleaves to give two new, smooth faces.

Demonstration 2.7. Cleaving a crystal

A Use a polystyrene model of a cubic crystal to show that it is easily split between two layers of 'atoms' in a direction parallel to a face of the crystal, Fig. 2.8.

Fig. 2.8

B The cleavage of a large calcite crystal may be demonstrated as in Fig. 2.9 by holding a trimming knife (e.g. Stanley) so that it is parallel to any face of the crystal and hitting it sharply with

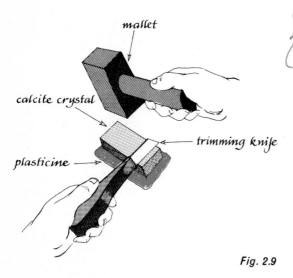

mallet

calcite crystal

trimming knife

plasticine

Fig. 2.9

a hammer or a mallet. (A single-edged razor-blade can also be used but is less satisfactory.)

Smash the slice of calcite obtained and look at the shapes of the large numbers of tiny fragments produced.

Use is made of crystal cleavage when the rough diamonds found in nature are cut along their natural planes at an early stage in the production of gems. Later they are cut, not along natural faces, but so that they reflect as much light as possible and sparkle brightly.

A crystalline substance which cleaves very easily is graphite. We know its atoms are

arranged in layers which slide readily over each other. As a result, graphite is useful as a lubricant to reduce friction between moving metal surfaces and it is also suitable as the 'lead' in pencils because it transfers easily on to paper.

An interesting point about diamond and graphite is that both are the same element, carbon. Although the atoms of a particular element are usually arranged in one way, this is not always so. The very different properties of diamond and graphite are explained as being due to the different arrangement of the carbon atoms in the two substances. In diamond, one of the hardest substances known, they must be held together strongly. In graphite, although the atoms in each layer are not easily separated, the arrangement must be such that those in one layer are only loosely held to those above and below it. The shape of a diamond crystal is shown in Fig. 2.10.

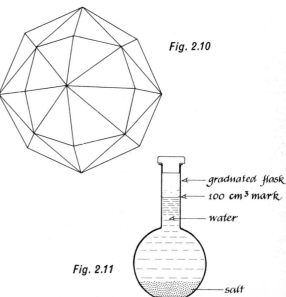

Fig. 2.10

graduated flask

100 cm³ mark

water

Fig. 2.11

salt

Crystals dissolving

Experiment 2.8. Watching salt crystals dissolve under a microscope

Put a few salt crystals on a microscope slide and observe them through the microscope. Add a few drops of water from a dropping-tube and watch the crystals dissolve.

Can you suggest a possible explanation, using the particle model, of what happens when crystals dissolve?

Demonstration 2.9. Volume change when salt dissolves in water

Put 30 g of salt crystals in a 100 cm³ graduated flask. Cover the salt with water and gently swirl the flask so that trapped air bubbles escape. Add water up to the 100 cm³ mark and note that most of the salt is still present, Fig. 2.11. Shake the flask until the salt dissolves. Is the level of the salt solution at the 100 cm³ mark? What does the result suggest about the packing together of water particles and salt particles when they are mixed?

Q. 2.2 Mr Y. Howe is an intelligent old gentleman who never did physics at school and is always asking questions. He cannot see any connexion between crystals and the idea of atoms. Write a few sentences on each of the following topics, explaining to him how they can be understood if you think of crystals as being built of atoms: (*a*) crystal shapes; (*b*) crystal sizes and growth; (*c*) crystal cleavage; (*d*) crystals dissolving.

Growing a large crystal

If crystals are grown rapidly a confused mass of thousands of tiny crystals is obtained. This happened when you grew hypo and salt crystals in earlier experiments. Under proper conditions a large crystal can be grown if a small, well-shaped seed crystal is first produced and then allowed to grow *slowly* in a saturated solution of the substance.

Experiment 2.10. Growing a copper sulphate crystal

Fill one-third of a test-tube with hot water and place it in a beaker of boiling water. Make a saturated solution by adding powdered copper sulphate to the test-tube until no more will dissolve, Fig. 2.12*a*. Remove the test-tube, filter the

Fig. 2.12

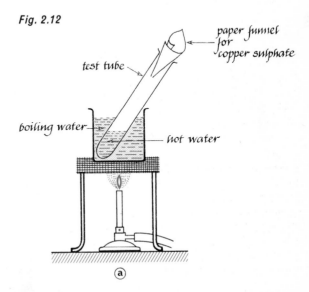

test tube
paper funnel for copper sulphate
boiling water
hot water

(a)

Fig. 2.12—contd.

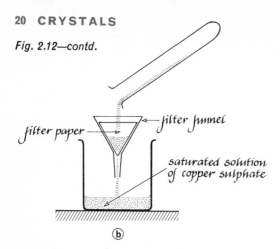

filter paper — filter funnel

saturated solution of copper sulphate

(b)

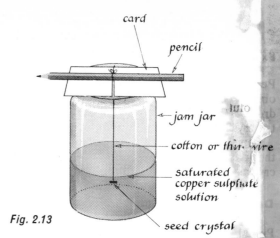

card

pencil

jam jar

cotton or thin wire

saturated copper sulphate solution

seed crystal

Fig. 2.13

solution into a clean beaker, Fig. 2.12*b* and leave it to evaporate to dryness in a dust-free cupboard.

For the seed crystal, choose the largest, best-shaped one in the beaker with the help of a magnifying glass if necessary. Tie a length of cotton or thin wire to it. This requires patience and nimble fingers. Suspend it from a pencil in a jam-jar containing a saturated solution of copper sulphate, cover with a piece of card, Fig. 2.13, and leave in a cupboard where the temperature is fairly constant.

At intervals of a few days inspect the crystal and if any small irregular growths have appeared on its faces remove them by rubbing with very fine sandpaper. Wash the crystal under cold water. Some powdered copper sulphate should be added from time to time to keep the solution saturated.

Crystal growing is often done better at home using the *falling temperature method* whereby the crystal is placed in the saturated solution (slightly warmed) at night and removed in the

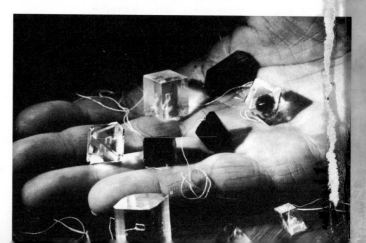

Fig. 2.14

morning. This helps to ensure that the crystal is never in the solution when the temperature rises. Otherwise if the solution became unsaturated the crystal would dissolve. In summer, the temperature does not fall so much indoors at night and the solution can be placed outside in a shed or garage.

Large alum crystals can also be grown fairly easily. Fig. 2.14 shows a variety of crystals grown in a school laboratory.

Molecules

The crystals studied so far have been fairly obviously crystalline in the way most people understand. However, our particle models of crystals have suggested that what really makes something crystalline is the orderly arrangement of its building blocks. They must have a regular pattern. Until now we have considered atoms as the only building blocks but there are others and we shall now see how these enable us to extend the idea of the crystalline state to almost all solids, even fibres like wool and nylon.

A compound contains at least two elements and so every tiny particle of a compound must consist of two or more different atoms. The smallest particle of a compound which cannot be broken up and still be that compound is called a *molecule*. Taking water as an example, one molecule of water is made up of two atoms of hydrogen and one atom of oxygen, Fig. 2.15a. Molecules of compounds found in living material are very complex and may contain many thousands of atoms. A molecule is thus a group of atoms.

The smallest particle of an element is an atom but the atoms of many elements do not appear to go around alone. For example, the atoms of hydrogen and oxygen are usually found in pairs and we can therefore talk about the molecules of these gases. A molecule of hydrogen or oxygen thus consists of two identical atoms, Fig. 2.15b.

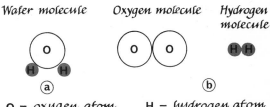

Fig. 2.15

To sum up, a molecule is a group of atoms which may be all different although not necessarily. The term molecule is a more general one than atom and is frequently used when we talk about the basic building blocks of matter without having any particular substance in mind.

Plastics and polymers

Plastics are now a feature of everyday life. Their properties vary from the toughness of polythene, through the glass-like qualities of 'Perspex' to the sheerness of nylon fabric. But despite their differences they are all members of the group known as *polymers*.

Polymers are giant molecules made by joining together large numbers of smaller molecules into a long chain. Among the many natural polymers is cellulose. It is present in all plants; its long, tough fibres provide stiffness and strength

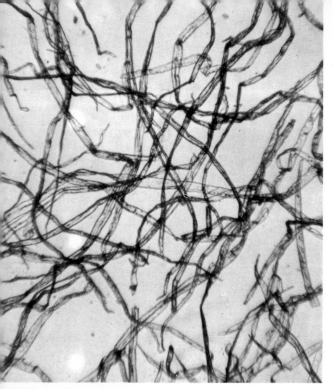

Fig. 2.16

fibres by an electron microscope (a very powerful type of magnifying instrument) shows that the cellulose molecules forming the fibre lie close together side by side along part of their length, Fig. 2.18. In many other natural fibres such as

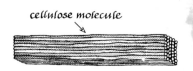

cellulose molecule

cellulose fibre magnified a million times

Fig. 2.18

wool, cotton and hair it is found that the long chain molecules are similarly arranged and form bundles in the fibre rather like wires in a cable. In a way then the molecules are arranged in an orderly fashion and are not jumbled like cooked spaghetti. We may therefore think of the fibres as having a 'crystalline' structure even though they may be soft and do not sparkle.

Cellulose from wood-pulp is the essential ingredient of paper; perhaps you saw the long cellulose fibres when you looked at a piece of paper under the microscope in Experiment 1.2. Cellulose is also the raw material for cellulose acetate, a plastic used to make photographic film, cellophane, ball-point pens, spectacle frames and motor-car paint.

Cellulose is a natural polymer: artificial polymers can now be made from substances derived from coal and crude oil. When fibres of artificial polymers, e.g. nylon, 'Terylene' and 'Courtelle', are manufactured, they have the greatest strength when crystalline, that is when their molecules are as nearly parallel as possible.

to stems, roots and leaves, Fig. 2.16. Every molecule of cellulose, Fig. 2.17, consists of a long chain of from a few hundred to several thousand glucose sugar molecules. Examination of the

Fig. 2.17

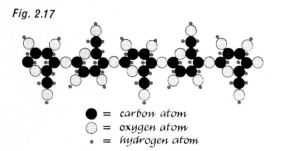

● = carbon atom
◉ = oxygen atom
· = hydrogen atom

Fig. 2.19

Fig. 2.20

Figs. 2.19 and 2.20 show nylon at its most sheer and at its toughest. One of the commonest man-made polymers is the plastic known as polythene used to make washing-up bowls, buckets, food containers and wrappers, etc. Polyethylene, to give it its full name, is made from ethylene, a gas obtained from crude oil. In one process the ethylene molecules are heated under very high

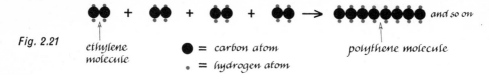

Fig. 2.21

ethylene
molecule

● = carbon atom

. = hydrogen atom

polythene molecule

and so on

pressure and combine with one another, Fig. 2.21.

Fig. 2.22 shows polythene granules before they are softened to make various products. Bouncing putty, which we mentioned on p. 8, is a silicone polymer.

Fig. 2.22

A chemical garden

Mix waterglass (from chemists and used for preserving eggs) with three times its volume of warm water. Pour the solution into a jam jar having a layer of sand at the bottom.

Allow things to settle and then drop in crystals of cobalt chloride, alum, hypo, copper sulphate, magnesium sulphate, iron sulphate and an iron nail. A crystal of potassium bichromate will give the solution a lovely pale green colour.

Watch the 'garden' grow. Cobalt chloride forms 'trees' very quickly but the other crystals will take a day or two.

British Aircraft Corporation One-Eleven flight deck. The instruments and controls on the various panels are within easy reach of either pilot

3 Measuring

The need to measure

In everyday life we are always having to make measurements. The distances between places have to be known for road sign-posts and times have to be measured before bus and railway time-tables can be drawn up. At present electrical wire and dress materials are sold by the yard, petrol by the gallon and sugar by the pound. However, as the metric system is adopted in Britain these will be replaced by the metre, the litre and the kilogramme. All are called standards or *units* of measurement.

Measurements are of the greatest importance to scientists and engineers. For example, they may have to measure how strong the casing of a car tyre is by dropping a load on it, Fig. 3.1, or, using a Geiger-Müller tube, measure the thickness of the zinc coating remaining on an electricity pylon which has been corroded by the atmosphere, Fig. 3.2. Many kinds of measuring instruments have been designed. The instrument panel of a car contains quite a variety. As well as the speedometer and the distance meter, there is the petrol gauge, the oil-pressure gauge, and a thermometer to give the temperature of the cooling water.

The flight-deck (cockpit) of the BAC One-Eleven bus jet air-craft is shown on p. 25. The multitude of meters keeps the pilot informed of how all the vital systems in the aircraft are behaving. An astronaut too has to place a great deal of reliance on his instruments. Fig. 3.3 shows American astronaut Scott Carpenter at the controls of his space capsule.

Q. 3.1 Name some units of measurement other than those mentioned in this section.

Q. 3.2 What different kinds of information do you think a pilot should have to fly his plane safely? Find out the names of some of the instruments he uses.

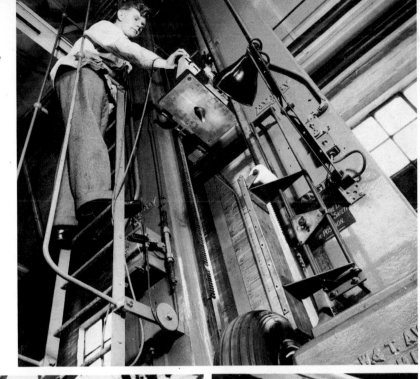

Fig. 3.1

Figs. 3.2 and 3.3

The metre

In the *metric system*, which is the one we will use from now on, the unit of length is the *metre* (shortened to m).

    Originally the metre was taken as one ten-millionth of the distance from the North Pole through Paris to the Equator, Fig. 3.4. Nowadays

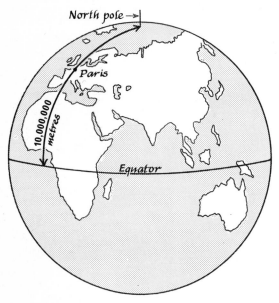

Fig. 3.4

it is defined, for all but the most accurate scientific work, as the distance between two marks on a bar of a platinum alloy kept at a fixed temperature. The standard metre is kept near Paris and copies of it are used in other countries for checking national standards.

The metre is divided into centimetres (cm) and millimetres (mm).

$$1 \text{ centimetre} = \frac{1}{100} \text{ metre} = 0{\cdot}01 \text{ metre}$$

$$1 \text{ millimetre} = \frac{1}{1000} \text{ metre} = 0{\cdot}001 \text{ metre}$$

$$= \frac{1}{10} \text{ centimetre} = 0{\cdot}1 \text{ centimetre}.$$

Examine a metre ruler which is marked in centimetres and millimetres and then answer the following questions.

Q. 3.3 How many millimetres are there in (*a*) 1 cm, (*b*) 3 cm, (*c*) 5½ cm (in decimals this is 5·5 cm), (*d*) 10 cm?

Q. 3.4 What are these lengths in metres (*a*) 400 cm, (*b*) 750 cm, (*c*) 1200 cm, (*d*) 50 cm?

Q. 3.5 How many (*a*) centimetres, (*b*) milli-metres, are there in 1 metre?

Q. 3.6 Why is a bar of a platinum alloy used for the standard metre rather than say a steel bar, and why is it at a fixed temperature?

Measuring lengths

Experiment 3.1. Measuring lengths

A Use a metre rule to measure the length of your shoe, your handspan, i.e. the distance between the tip of your thumb and the tip of your little finger when farthest apart, the length and width of a sheet of paper, an average walking pace, the length and width of the laboratory or classroom. Make sure you read the rule from directly above, see Fig. 3.5.

B To test your 'metric-mindedness' try guessing some lengths to the nearest centimetre and then check each one with a ruler. You might start with the breadth of your hand, the length of your middle finger, the length and width of a bench or desk, the height of the laboratory or classroom.

a 'histogram'. The start of one is shown in Fig. 3.6 where you can see from the shaded column that 5 pupils are 135 cm or more tall but are less than 140 cm.

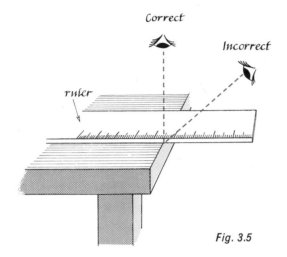

Fig. 3.5

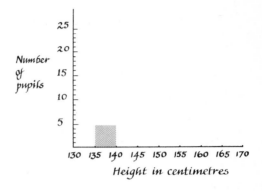

Fig. 3.6

Although a great deal of scientific work has to be very accurate, there are occasions when estimates or rough measurements such as you have just been making are perfectly satisfactory. This often happens with scientific matters in everyday life. For example, if a new town is being planned, the engineer responsible for the electricity supply needs to know whether the population will be 10,000 or 100,000. If it is the latter then he will not be greatly worried if it turns out to be 98,000 or 102,000 and he certainly does not need to be told that there will be exactly 100,023 people.

It is interesting, especially to health authorities, to see how heights vary among people. An easy way of showing this is by means of a chart called

Experiment 3.2. Measuring your own height

Measure your height to the *nearest centimetre* and from the results for the whole class make a histogram by drawing blocks so that the top of each block shows the number of pupils whose heights are between certain values.

Accuracy and averages

In making measurements scientists have to consider what accuracy they require and how far it can be achieved with the particular instrument(s) used. Suppose you wish to measure the width of a box which has to be moved through a doorway 80·0 cm wide. If a quick measurement shows that

Fig. 3.7

Fig. 3.8

the box is about 71 cm wide this accuracy would be sufficient. But if it was found to be roughly 80 cm then a more accurate determination would be necessary. Using a ruler marked in milli-metres we could perhaps say whether the width of the box was 79·9 cm, 80·0 cm or 80·1 cm. It is doubtful if an answer of say 79·73 cm could be justified using such a ruler. This would be an 'over-accurate' result.

Scientists are seldom satisfied with one measurement for a particular quantity and often take the average of several readings. Suppose that ten measurements of the width of a bench in cm were

102, 100, 101, 103, 101, 100, 103, 100, 101, 102

The average is found by adding the measure-ments together and then dividing by 10. The answer is 1013/10=101·3 cm. However, the measurements were made to the nearest centi-metre and the average has been given to the first decimal place. This is claiming a greater accuracy than the original measurements justify and is something that we should avoid. The average to

the nearest centimetre is 101 cm. If the average had been 101·5 or any value up to 101·9, this would have been taken as 102 cm.

Measuring large distances

Long distances are generally measured indirectly and in the metric system are expressed in kilo-metres (km).

1 kilometre=1000 metres=($\frac{5}{8}$ mile approxi-mately)

1. USING A WHEEL

One method is to count the number of times a wheel has to turn to cover the distance. Curved lines can be measured in this way. Two instru-ments which work on this principle are the road measurer, Fig. 3.7, and the map measurer, Fig. 3.8. The distance measuring device on a car also works in the same way and although it is marked to show distance it really counts the number of turns made by the car's wheels.

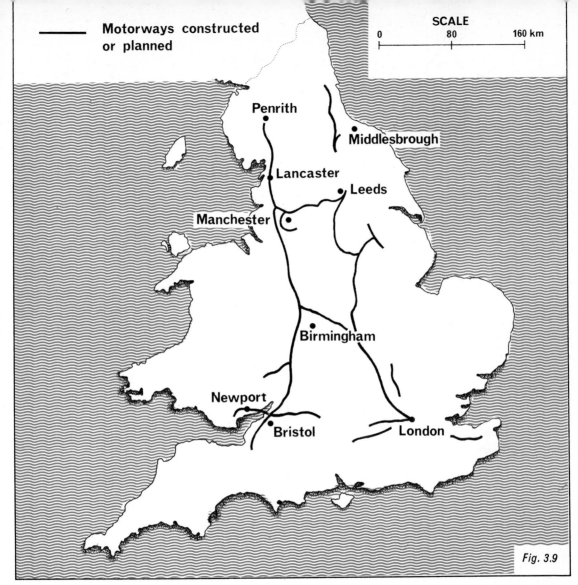

SCALE

0   80   160 km

Motorways constructed or planned

Penrith

Middlesbrough

Lancaster

Leeds

Manchester

Birmingham

Newport

Bristol

London

Fig. 3.9

Experiment 3.3. Measuring distance on a map
Estimate from the map of Fig. 3.9 what the distance would be by motorway from London to Lancaster. Use a piece of cotton or a wire first of all and then try with a coin. The scale of the map is given on it.

31

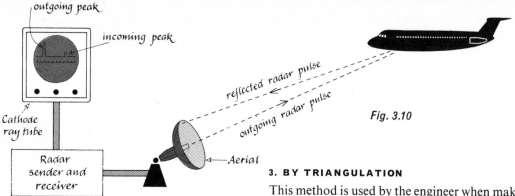

outgoing peak

incoming peak

reflected radar pulse

outgoing radar pulse

Fig. 3.10

Cathode
ray tube

Radar
sender and
receiver

Aerial

2. BY RADAR

Distances can be measured by sending out short bursts of radio waves from an aerial so that they bounce back to the aerial from the object to be located, usually an aircraft. The outgoing and incoming bursts are made to cause peaks on a cathode ray tube (similar to a television tube) on which times are marked, Fig. 3.10. Knowing the time between the two peaks and also that radio waves travel with the speed of light (300,000 kilometres per second) the distance can be worked out.

3. BY TRIANGULATION

This method is used by the engineer when making a survey. Suppose that the width OD of a broad river, across which a bridge is to be built, has to be measured. O is a landmark on the opposite bank and BL a suitable base-line on the near bank, Fig. 3.11a. The length of BL is measured with a measuring tape or chain and found to be 450 m. From B, angle OBL is found to be 60° and from L, angle OLB is 45°.

A triangle $O'B'L'$ is then drawn on paper so that $B'L'$ represents BL to a certain scale, say 1 cm to 100 m, and so that angle $O'B'L'$ is 60° and angle $O'L'B'$ is 45°, Fig. 3.11b. From triangle $O'B'L'$, $O'D'$ can be found. If $O'D'$ is 3 cm, then the actual distance OD is 300 m.

Astronomers could use the same method to find the distance of the moon from the earth. B and L in this case would be two observatories a known distance apart on the earth and O

Fig. 3.11

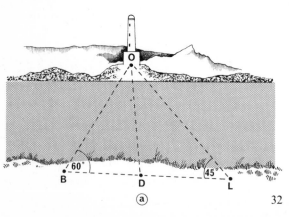

O

60°

B

D

45°

L

(a)

O'

60°

B'

D'

45°

L'

(b)

would be a point on the moon. In practice, however, more complicated procedures are followed.

Q. 3.7 Suppose you had to find the length of a running track by using a bicycle wheel, what measurement would you have to know about the wheel and how would you obtain the length of the track?

Q. 3.8 In the radar method of finding distance, the time between the peaks is $\frac{1}{500}$ second for a particular object. How far is the object from the aerial?

Q. 3.9 Mr Y. Howe has a tall tree at the bottom of his garden and wants to know how high it is. He asks you to help him. What measurements would you make and how would you obtain the height of the tree from them? (You cannot climb the tree.)

Powers of 10 shorthand

The distance of the moon from the earth is about 400,000 km and of the sun about 150,000,000 km. To make these and other such numbers less awkward to write and read, scientists use a shorthand method. It works like this.

$$40=4\times10 \qquad \text{and is written } 4\times10^1.$$
$$400=4\times100=4\times10\times10$$
$$\text{and is written } 4\times10^2.$$
$$4000=4\times1000=4\times10\times10\times10$$
$$\text{and is written } 4\times10^3.$$

The small figures 1, 2 and 3 are called *powers* of 10 and tell us how many 10s should be multiplied together. The distance to the moon is $4\times100,000$ km and in powers of 10 shorthand it is written 4×10^5 km.

The sun–earth distance can be written as $15\times10,000,000$ km$=15\times10^7$ km. Usually, however, scientists give their answers in the form of a power of 10 number multiplied by another number which has just one figure before the decimal point. The sun–earth distance would therefore be $1\cdot5\times100,000,000$ km$=1\cdot5\times10^8$ km.

Writing numbers in this way has another advantage. A scientist knows that his measurements can never be absolutely accurate because neither he nor his instruments are perfect, but he usually has a good idea of how wrong he may be. He shows his uncertainty by only giving in his measurement or result as many figures after the decimal point as he believes his accuracy deserves. For example, the speed of light has now been measured so accurately that it is stated to be $2\cdot997925\times10^5$ kilometres per second. This means that scientists are sure about the first six figures and, although they think the last figure is probably 5, it might be 4 or 6.

Small fractions can also be represented by the powers of 10 method. Here are some examples:

Fraction	$\frac{1}{100}$	$\frac{2}{10,000}$	$\frac{1}{5,000}$	$\frac{3}{200,000}$
Powers of 10	$\frac{1}{10^2}$	$\frac{2}{10^4}$	$\frac{1}{5\times10^3}$	$\frac{3}{2\times10^5}$

Q. 3.10 (*a*) Write the following numbers in powers of 10 form, putting one figure before the decimal point. (Example: $534,000=5\cdot34\times10^5$.) 1,000,000; 9,000; 2,500; 186,000; 437,000,000. (*b*) What are the following in words: 10^3; 3×10^6; $5\cdot8\times10^4$; $1\cdot52\times10^2$; $1\cdot86\times10^5$? (*c*) Write these fractions in powers of 10 form:

$$\frac{1}{1000}; \frac{7}{100,000}; \frac{1}{100,000,000}; \frac{5}{60,000}.$$

Measuring small lengths

Short lengths can be measured with special instruments but we will try to use a little ingenuity and make do with a ruler.

Experiment 3.4. Measuring thickness

Use a ruler marked in millimetres.

A Measure the thickness of *one* penny. How could you get a more accurate result?

B If you have found how to do *A* accurately you should be able to find the thickness of one page of this book using the same method.

C Wind a piece of wire ten times round a pencil so that there are no spaces between the turns,

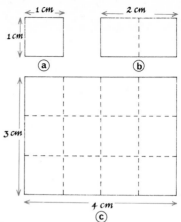

Fig. 3.13

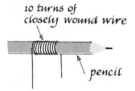

Fig. 3.12

Fig. 3.12. Can you now make a measurement with the ruler which will enable you to find the thickness (diameter) of the wire fairly accurately?

Q. 3.11 Think carefully about this question. How many grooves are there in, say, a 'pop' record? Can you think of a way of measuring fairly accurately the width of such a groove?

Measuring areas

A football or a hockey pitch occupies a certain *area* of land. The longer and the wider the pitch the greater is its area. In Fig. 3.13*a* a square having sides 1 cm long is shown. It has an area of 1 *square centimetre* (shortened to 1 cm²). In Fig. 3.13*b* the rectangle shown measures 2 cm by 1 cm. It has an area of 2 cm² since it is the same as two squares each of area 1 cm². The rectangle in Fig. 3.13*c* has length 4 cm and breadth 3 cm and contains $4 \times 3 = 12$ squares, each of 1 cm². It has an area of 12 cm².

To find the area of a square or a rectangle it is not necessary to divide it up into squares of area 1 cm² as we have been doing. We can simply multiply the length by the breadth. For a square or a rectangle

$$\text{AREA} = \text{LENGTH} \times \text{BREADTH}.$$

Area is measured in square centimetres, square metres, square kilometres, etc., since two distances are multiplied together.

How can the areas of shapes other than squares and rectangles be found? An estimate may be obtained by dividing up the area as before into

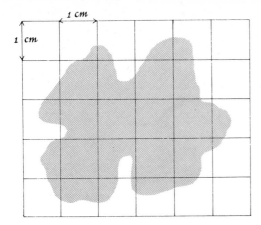

Fig. 3.14

use one of its sub-multiples—the *cubic centimetre* (written cm³) which is the volume of a cube the edges of which are each 1 cm long, Fig. 3.15.

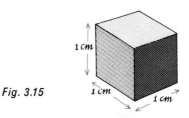

Fig. 3.15

squares each of area, say, 1 cm², Fig. 3.14. Incomplete squares having an area of ½ cm² or more are counted as complete squares and those of area less than ½ cm² ignored.

Experiment 3.5. Measuring the area of England and Wales

Using tracing-paper draw the outline of England and Wales from the map on page 31. Find the area enclosed by your outline in square centimetres. From the scale of the map estimate the actual area of England and Wales in square kilometres. Find out the accepted value.

Volume: solids and liquids

The volume of a piece of matter is the amount of space it occupies. The metric unit of volume is the cubic metre but as this is rather large we will

1. REGULAR SOLIDS

The volume of a regularly-shaped object such as a box can be calculated by measuring its length, breadth and height. Thus the volume of the box in Fig. 3.16a is 4 cm × 3 cm × 2 cm = 24 cm³. We

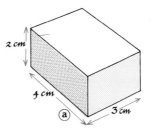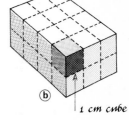

Fig. 3.16

can see that this is so from Fig. 3.16b in which the same box has been divided up into cubes each of volume 1 cm³. The volume equals the number of these unit cubes. For a cubical or rectangular object

$$\text{VOLUME} = \text{LENGTH} \times \text{BREADTH} \times \text{HEIGHT}.$$

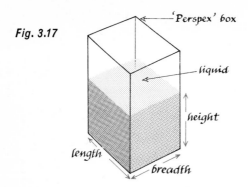

Fig. 3.17

'Perspex' box

liquid

height

length

breadth

2. LIQUIDS

The volume of a liquid can be found by pouring it into a rectangular 'Perspex' box and measuring its length, breadth and height, Fig. 3.17. Another method uses a measuring cylinder marked in volume units, Fig. 3.18. The surface of water is curved, forming a meniscus, and when making a reading the eye must be level with the *bottom* of this meniscus, as shown. The meniscus formed by mercury is curved in the opposite direction to that of water and most other liquids and in this case the *top* of the meniscus is read.

Liquid volumes are often measured in litres.

1 litre (l)=1000 cubic centimetres.

Sometimes one-thousandth of a litre, one milli-litre (1 ml), is used instead of 1 cm³.

Experiment 3.6. Measuring a volume of water

Use a rectangular 'Perspex' box or a measuring cylinder to find the number of cubic centimetres of water a milk or lemonade bottle holds.

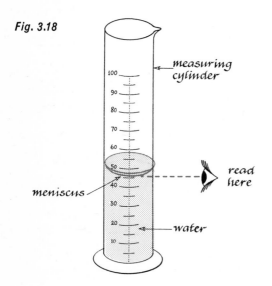

Fig. 3.18

measuring cylinder

100
90
80
70
60
50
40
30
20
10

meniscus

read here

water

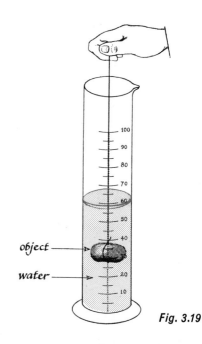

100
90
80
70
60
50
40
30
20
10

object

water

Fig. 3.19

3. IRREGULAR SOLIDS

Most solids have odd shapes and the volume of such an irregular solid cannot be calculated easily from length measurements.

Experiment 3.7. Measuring the volume of a glass stopper or a pebble

Half fill a measuring cylinder with water and read the volume. Lower the object so that it is all in the water and read the new volume, Fig. 3.19. Calculate the volume of the object.

Fig. 3.20

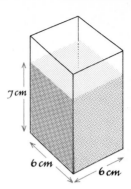

Problems on volume

Q. 3.12 A wooden block measures 5 cm × 4 cm × 3 cm. How many cubical blocks 1 cm × 1 cm × 1 cm would be required to make a block having the same volume as the wooden one?

Q. 3.13 A glass block measures 10 cm × 2 cm × 2 cm. What is its volume? How many cubical blocks each 2 cm × 2 cm × 2 cm are there in it?

Q. 3.14 How many packets of frozen peas each 10 cm × 10 cm × 4 cm can be stored in the compartment of a deep freeze measuring 40 cm × 40 cm × 20 cm?

Q. 3.15 A 'Perspex' box has a 6 cm square base and contains water to a height of 7 cm, Fig. 3.20.
(*a*) What is the volume of the water?
(*b*) A stone is lowered into the water so as to be completely covered and the water rises to a height of 9 cm. What is the volume of the stone?

Q. 3.16 How would you find the volume of (*a*) a lollipop, (*b*) a small cork?

Q. 3.17 A cubical box of side 1 cm holds 64 ball-bearings; 64 drops of water from a dropping-tube also fill it completely.
(*a*) What, as a fraction of a centimetre, is the volume of 1 drop of water?
(*b*) Is the volume of 1 ball-bearing larger, smaller or the same? Why?

Measuring time

Time is one of the basic ideas in science and has frequently to be measured. Whereas we can store, say, our unit of length, we cannot keep a standard piece of time. Time is just not like that.

The unit of time which we shall most often use is the *second*. This, as you know, is a certain fraction of a day, a day being the time for the earth to complete one revolution. Unfortunately days are not all of exactly the same length but this is only important in more advanced work.

With a little practice you can become quite good at estimating an interval of time. Seconds may be counted by saying at normal talking speed 'Hundred and 1, hundred and 2, etc.'

Experiment 3.8 Estimating time intervals

A Count quietly to yourself up to 30 by the method suggested above and check against a watch or clock having a seconds hand.

B Estimate the time in seconds between two hand-claps made by your partner.

C Estimate how long it takes someone to walk the length of the laboratory or room three times.

D Get someone to estimate how long you can hold your breath.

E Estimate the time it takes a penny to fall from a height of 1 metre to the floor.

A clock is necessary for accurate time measurements. An early type was the candle clock. Can you suggest how it worked? Another was the hour-glass consisting of two glass bulbs, one containing sand, connected by a small hole and similar to some present-day egg-timers. How do you think it worked?

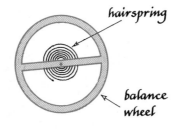

Fig. 3.21

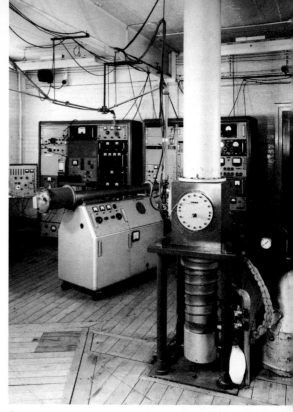

Fig. 3.22. Atomic clock at the National Physical Laboratory (N.P.L.)

Most watches and small clocks have a balance-wheel and hair spring, Fig. 3.21. The balance wheel is kept oscillating to and fro by an arrangement attached to the main spring and it always takes the same time to make one oscillation. The hands are connected to gears driven by the balance wheel. Electric clocks rely on very rapid 'oscillations of electric current' to drive their hands.

Very accurate atomic clocks have now been made, Fig. 3.22, which depend on vibrations in ammonia molecules and caesium atoms. These clocks are reliable to one second in 300 years but they are very complex.

Expanded polystyrene block. Made by heating polystyrene powder which is a plastic having a long chain molecule and is obtained from chemicals in crude oil

4 Weighing

CHAPTER FOUR **WEIGHING**

Weight and mass

We all find out at a very early age that unless an object is supported it will fall. We explain this behaviour by saying that the earth is pulling the object to its centre. An object such as a lump of lead is pulled down strongly while a feather is only pulled down weakly —we can feel this with our arm muscles. The lead is said to have a big weight and the feather a small weight. *Weight* or *the pull of the earth* on an object is a property of all matter, whether it is solid, liquid or gas.

As a way of measuring matter, weight is, unfortunately, not altogether satisfactory. For a particular object, it can be different in different places. For example, a bag of apples is pulled more by the earth at sea-level than it is on the top of a high mountain and so its weight is, therefore, greater at sea-level. There is, however, the same amount of stuff present wherever the bag is. This 'something' which remains the same and does not depend on the position of the object is called by scientists, the *mass* of the object. We will not trouble too much at present about the difference between weight and mass but we shall want to measure mass. This is most conveniently done by 'weighing' the object on a balance—which is just a bit confusing.

The unit of mass is the *kilogramme* (kg) and is the mass of a piece of platinum alloy, kept like the standard metre, near Paris. The kilogramme is divided into grammes (g) and

$$1000 \text{ grammes} = 1 \text{ kilogramme}$$

$$\therefore 1 \text{ gramme} = \frac{1}{1000} \text{ kilogramme}$$

Weight is not measured in kilogrammes or grammes but in other units we will discuss later in the course. You may, however, find that packets of butter etc. are marked 'Net *weight* 500 g'; this is incorrect and should be 'Net *mass* 500 g'.

Weighing solids

There are many kinds of balances for 'weighing' matter but one of the quickest and simplest to use is the lever-arm type (also called the Butchart balance). You may have met it earlier in the course, Fig. 4.1.

Fig. 4.1

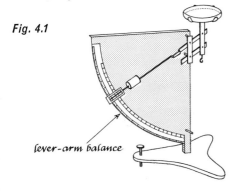

lever-arm balance

Some lever-arm balances are double-range instruments (0–250 g and 0–1000 g are common ranges) and a simple adjustment may have to be made on the balance to give readings on the range desired. To avoid reading the wrong scale it is a good idea to cover the scale which is not to be used with masking tape.

Experiment 4.1. Weighing blocks of the same size

Using a lever-arm balance reading on the 0–1000 g scale, find the masses of blocks (size 5 cm × 4 cm × 3 cm is suitable) of softwood, hardwood, aluminium, iron, paraffin wax and expanded polystyrene. A block of the last-mentioned material of the size suggested presents a difficulty. How can you overcome it?

Roughly how many times heavier is a block of iron than one of aluminium of the same size? Make comparisons of the other materials.

Density

A bunker, stated by a reliable manufacturer to hold 1000 kg of coal, was purchased by our friend Mr Y. Howe, who decided to store coke in it. He ordered 1000 kg of coke but when it was delivered he found to his great annoyance that the bunker would only take about 700 kg, Fig. 4.2. Was he misled by the manufacturer? Perhaps after we have done the next experiment we can decide.

Fig. 4.2

Experiment 4.2. Weighing blocks of different sizes

Find the masses of blocks of various materials of different sizes using a lever-arm balance. Also measure them with a ruler *marked in centimetres only*. Draw up a table for your results as shown, but add an extra column at the end.

Material	Mass g	Length cm	Breadth cm	Height cm	Volume cm³
Lead	550	5	5	2	50
Aluminium		5	5	8	200
Glass					

If the aluminium and lead blocks with the measurements given in the table were used you have probably found that their masses are about the same, yet we normally think of lead as being 'heavier' than aluminium. However, to make a fair comparison of what in everyday language is often called 'heaviness', we must take into account the *volume* of each material as well as its *mass*. To do this we compare the masses of equal volumes of the materials; a volume of 1 cm³ is often considered.

If a volume of 50 cm³ of lead has a mass of 550 g, then 1 cm³ of lead has a mass $\frac{1}{50}$ of 550 g, that is $\frac{550}{50} = 11$ g. The mass of 1 cm³ of a material is called the *density* of the material and so the density of lead is 11 g per cm³. Notice that the *unit* of density used here is the *gramme per cubic centimetre*.

Work out the density of aluminium in g per cm³ and compare it with that of lead. Work out the densities of the blocks of all the other materials used in the experiment and write your answers in the last column of the table.

Q. 4.1 If a material is bulky but has a small mass its density is high/low (state which). What can you say about the density of the material shown on p. 39?

Q. 4.2 Mr Y. Howe says he now thinks he knows why he cannot get 1000 kg of coke into his bunker designed for 1000 kg of coal. It is because 'coal is *heavier* than coke'. Is he absolutely correct? Can you give him a better explanation?

Questions on density

You may have noticed when working out densities in Experiment 4.2 that the answer is obtained by dividing the mass by the volume.

$$\text{DENSITY} = \frac{\text{MASS}}{\text{VOLUME}}.$$

If we use D for density, M for mass and V for volume then

$$D = \frac{M}{V} \qquad (1)$$

Multiplying *both* sides of this expression by V does not make it any less true and we get

$$V \times D = V \times \frac{M}{V}$$

The Vs cancel out on the top and bottom of the right side of the expression giving

$$V \times D = M \text{ or}$$
$$M = D \times V \qquad (2)$$

This gives M if we know D and V. There is a third expression from which V can be calculated when D and M are known; it starts $V =$ Can you work it out?

Each one of these three expressions is called a *formula*. It is useful to remember $D=M/V$; the other two can be derived from it. When working out calculations the formulae (plural of formula) help to provide the answer quickly but it is also possible to arrive at it simply by thinking about what is meant by density.

Q. 4.3 What is the mass of (*a*) 1 cm³, (*b*) 5 cm³, (*c*) 10 cm³ of wood of density 0·5 g per cm³?

Q. 4.4 The density of gold is 19 g per cm³. Find the volume of (*a*) 38 g, (*b*) 95 g of gold.

Q. 4.5 Find the volume of a piece of ice of mass 9 g and density 0·9 g per cm³.

Q. 4.6 Knowing what you weigh in kilogrammes and taking the density of the human body as nearly 1 g per cm³ calculate your volume in litres.

Q. 4.7 Which is heavier, 1 kg of lead or 1 kg of feathers?

Q. 4.8 (*a*) How many aluminium cubes each 3 cm × 3 cm × 3 cm will fit into a cardboard box with inside measurements 12 cm × 9 cm × 6 cm?
(*b*) If the box when full has mass 1944 g, what is the mass of one aluminium cube? Say why the answer will not be *exactly* correct.

Weighing liquids

For fairly obvious reasons a liquid has to be weighed in the vessel containing it. However, the presence of the vessel introduces something which has usually to be taken into account. Think about this slight complication and decide how to overcome it before starting the next experiment.

Experiment 4.3. Finding the density of liquids

Find the mass of known volumes of methylated spirit, water and brine on a lever-arm balance. For the volume measurements use either a rectangular 'Perspex' box containing a certain

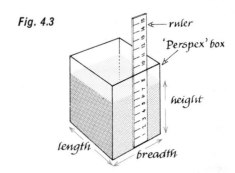

Fig. 4.3

depth of liquid, Fig. 4.3, or a measuring cylinder. Show your results in a table and work out the density of each liquid.

Liquid	Mass	Volume	Density
Methylated spirit			
Water			
Brine			

Q. 4.9 The density of a substance such as sand can be found as for a liquid by weighing a measured depth in a 'Perspex' box of known length and breadth. However, sand consists of particles packed together with spaces between them, rather like apples in a barrel.
(*a*) Will the measured volume be that of just the sand particles?
(*b*) Will the result be the density of the particles or that of the sand as a whole?

Q. 4.10 If water consists of very tiny, round molecules packed together how does their density compare with the density of water in bulk, i.e. with 1 g per cm³?

Weighing air

Nowadays we take the air for granted even if it is invisible. Of course, when it moves from one place to another as a wind we do notice its presence, just as we would if any other form of matter, solid or liquid, hit us.

Air has mass. Make a guess at the mass of air in the room. Before reading on, think about how we might try to weigh air.

Demonstration 4.4. Finding the density of air

A One procedure is to weigh a bottle or a large flask on a lever-arm balance, Fig. 4.4, and then to find the loss in mass when the air has been removed from it with a vacuum pump. The volume of the air can be found by filling the bottle or flask with water and pouring it into a rectangular 'Perspex' box or a measuring cylinder.

Try this method. Do you think it gives a reliable result using a lever-arm balance?

B Instead of removing air we can force more into a container and find the mass and volume of the 'extra' air. Pump air from a foot-pump into a large plastic container (about 30 cm × 30 cm × 30 cm) which has a tap, Fig. 4.5. About 100 strokes of the pump gives a reasonable mass

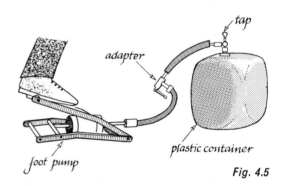

Fig. 4.5

tap

adapter

foot pump

plastic container

Fig. 4.4

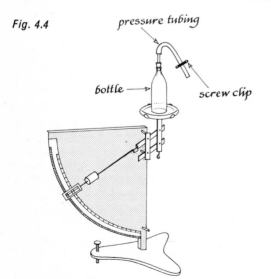

pressure tubing

bottle

screw clip

of air and is not likely to burst the container. (There is little danger if it does.) Weigh the container and extra air by *hanging it from a string on the hook under the balance pan*, Fig. 4.6. Make sure the container is not touching anything.

The extra air in the container has been squeezed; can its normal volume be found? Fig. 4.7 shows how, using a rectangular 'Perspex' box, 10 cm × 10 cm × 11 cm, we can release and collect 1 litre (1000 cm³) of air at a time. The box must

Demonstration 4.5. Solid carbon dioxide changing into carbon dioxide gas

Place several small chips of solid carbon dioxide ('dry ice') or two or three teaspoonfuls of carbon dioxide snow (made from a cylinder of the liquid, see Appendix 4, p. 110) inside a balloon. Flatten the balloon and tie the neck securely. The solid is at a temperature of $-78°C$ and changes to gas directly, missing out the liquid state. Observe what happens to the balloon.

Can you now offer an explanation in terms of the distance between molecules, of why gases are much less dense than solids and liquids? In view of your explanation how would you expect a gas to behave when it is squeezed?

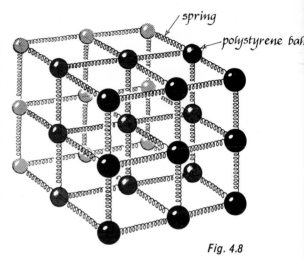

spring

polystyrene ball

Fig. 4.8

Experiment 4.6. Squeezing air

Draw back the piston of a bicycle pump or a nylon syringe. Place a finger over the outlet and push in the piston as far as you can. Did the volume of the air in the pump or syringe alter as you expected when it was squeezed?

Scientists believe that it is not only in gases that molecules are spaced apart but also in liquids and solids although the spacing is much closer in these cases. You may remember that when we studied crystals some salt was dissolved in a flask of water and a decrease in volume was noted (Demonstration 2.9). We might explain this as being due to the molecules of one substance fitting into the spaces between the other, to some extent at any rate.

Solids (and liquids) are therefore not quite so 'solid' as they look and it seems that they probably consist of atoms or molecules spaced a little apart. Perhaps the model shown in Fig. 4.8 is a better picture of the atoms in a solid than those we used when considering crystals which showed the atoms as touching one another.

Q. 4.13 1 cm³ of a certain liquid when boiled away completely gives 1000 cm³ of the vapour of the liquid.

(a) How does the number of molecules in the liquid compare with the number in the vapour?
(b) How many times farther apart are the molecules in the vapour compared with the distance apart in the liquid state?

Invisible forces

You may now be wondering how atoms can be kept in place in a solid if they are not in contact with each other. In the model, Fig. 4.8, springs

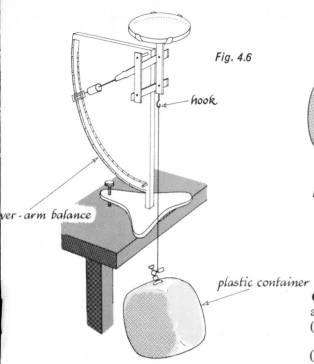

Fig. 4.6

hook

ver-arm balance

plastic container

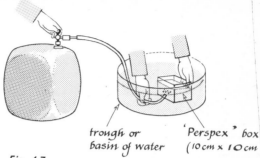

Fig. 4.7

trough or
basin of water

'Perspex' box
(10 cm x 10 cm

be full of water at the start of each collection and be held open end downwards in a sink or a large basin of water. It is easier if one person operates the tap on the container and the other holds the rubber tubing well under the box until it contains air to a height of 10 cm.

When the excess air has been released, weigh the container as before. Calculate the density of air in grammes per litre.

Q. 4.11 Using the result obtained for the density of air make a rough estimate of the mass of air in the room. Does it surprise you? How does it compare with your guess?

Q. 4.12 1 cm^3 of water weighs 1 g and 1 cm^3 of air weighs 12/10,000 g.
(a) What is the mass of (i) 1 litre of water, (ii) 1 litre of air?
(b) How many times is water denser than air?
(c) How many litres are there in 1 cubic metre?
(d) What is the mass of (i) 1 cubic metre of air. (ii) the air in a room 10 m × 5 m × 2 m?

Densities and molecules

In general the densities of solids and liquids a$_/$ several hundred times greater than those of a or any other gas. For example, in Q. 4.12b y probably found that water is more than 8 times denser than air. If water and air consist molecules of about the same size and ma how can we explain, in terms of molecules, big difference in their densities? The demonstration may help us.

hold the balls together but we think for atoms the forces are strong, short-range invisible ones. A force is a push or a pull such as you might exert using your muscles. Whilst we can see a muscular force being applied, some other important forces we study in physics are invisible. Can you name an invisible pull we have already considered? Later you will learn about other invisible forces but for the present we shall make a brief exploration of only one of them.

Experiment 4.7. Investigating magnetic forces

Using *two* magnets (preferably cylindrical) see what you can discover about magnetic forces. Are they pulls or pushes or both?

Demonstration 4.8. Floating magnets

Arrange several ring ceramic magnets[1] so that they float on a rod as shown in Fig. 4.9. Each of the top three magnets is kept in balance by two invisible forces, one pulling it down and the other pushing it up. What are the forces?

Perhaps the above demonstration will help you to see that something can be kept in a position of balance by two invisible forces. The invisible forces which atoms exert on each other are electrical in origin.

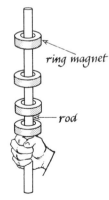

ring magnet

rod

Fig. 4.9

[1] Obtainable from Messrs E. J. Arnold Ltd, Butterley Street, Leeds 10; Type KN666.

Floating and sinking

Why do some solids float in water while others sink and why does a particular solid float in one liquid but sink in others?

Demonstration 4.9. Floating and sinking

Pour methylated spirit, water and mercury into three small beakers. Test small wooden and solid glass objects in each liquid. Draw a table like the one shown and insert in the appropriate space *S* for sinks and *F* for floats.

LIQUID → SOLID ↓	Methylated spirit (0·8 g per cm³)	Water (1 g per cm³)	Mercury (13·6 g per cm³)
Soft wood (about 0·5 g per cm³)			
Glass (2·5 g per cm³)			

The densities are given in parenthesis. Can you now answer in terms of density the questions at the beginning of the section?

Q. 4.14 Fig. 4.10 shows a bather reading a book whilst floating in the very salty water of the Dead Sea. Explain why so much of his body is out of the water.

Fig. 4.10

Figs. 4.11a and b

Q. 4.15 An iron nail sinks in water but a hollow iron ship weighing thousands of kilogrammes floats. Why?

Q. 4.16 The Swedish warship *Wasa*, which sank in a squall in Stockholm Harbour over three hundred years ago, was refloated in 1961. Fig. 4.11a shows the ship emerging from the water. Fig. 4.11b shows it in dock with three of its four buoyancy tanks. The tanks, full of water, were attached to the partly submerged ship which was then raised by pumping the water out of the tanks. Can you explain why this happened?

A simple balance

The ancient Egyptians knew something about weighing and produced a balance not unlike the scales still to be seen in some shops. Fig. 4.12 shows a simple balance which was discovered in an Egyptian tomb and is probably well over three thousand years old. What are the animals for?

Demonstration 4.10. Rough weighing of various objects

A very simple equal-arm balance is shown in Fig. 4.13.

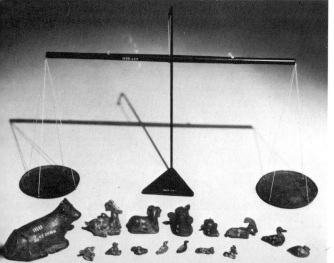

Fig. 4.12

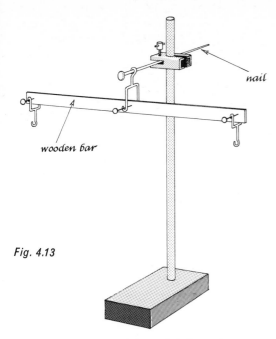

Fig. 4.13

A Weigh a parcel (about $\frac{1}{2}$ kg) to the nearest 100 g using 100 g slotted weights on a 100 g weight holder.
B Weigh a letter to the nearest 10 g using 10 g slotted weights.
C See if the balance will weigh a single hair.

A microbalance

Small light objects can be weighed using a very sensitive type of balance called a microbalance.

Experiment 4.11. Making a microbalance

The balance is shown in Fig. 4.14*a*. Make two small cuts at one end of a drinking-straw and form a scoop as in Fig. 4.14*b*. This acts as a pointer and also holds the object to be weighed so that it does not slide into the straw. Fit a small screw or bolt into the other end and find the rough balancing point by balancing the straw on the needle.

Push the needle through the straw and rest it on the U-shaped metal channel. A strip of card or a tongue depressor (from chemists), secured to a block of wood by elastic bands or supported by a clothes-peg, can be used for a scale. Adjust the screw until a suitable balance is obtained.

If the balance seems to want to swing about you should consider whether you have pushed

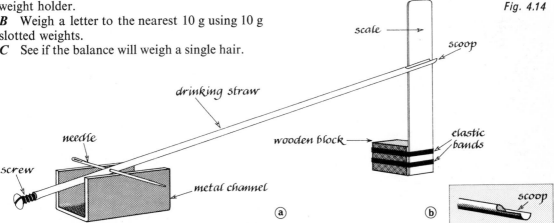

Fig. 4.14

the needle through the best place in the straw. Should it be through the widest part of the straw? If not, where? You may spoil several straws before getting the position right but it is worth persevering and making a good balance.

Experiment 4.12. Using a microbalance

You probably have your own ideas about small objects to weigh but here are a few suggestions: a hair, one or two crystals of granulated sugar, 1 or 2 cm of thread.

How about weights? Can you think of a way of cutting up sheets of graph-paper[1] and using the small pieces as weights to mark the scale? This is called calibrating the balance. Calibrate the balance using 'paper weights'. If you find your balance is so insensitive that one tiny 'paper weight' hardly deflects it then you should again consider the position of the needle in the straw. When things are satisfactory find what each object weighs, giving your answer as 'so many paper weights'.

To calculate the actual mass of each object in grammes is more difficult but if you weigh a bundle of 100 similar sheets of the graph paper all taped together, you may manage, with your teacher's help, to do this.

Experiment 4.13. Measuring the thickness of aluminium leaf

This cannot be done as for a sheet of paper by measuring the thickness of a pile of aluminium leaf. Screw up a piece of the leaf, say 2 cm × 2 cm, into a small ball and weigh it on your microbalance. Taking the density of aluminium as 3 g per cm³, we can calculate the thickness of the leaf. Suppose it is t cm, Fig. 4.15.

[1] Nuffield item 10B.

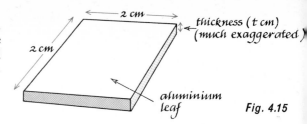

Fig. 4.15

Volume of leaf = length × breadth × thickness
$$= 2 \text{ cm} \times 2 \text{ cm} \times t \text{ cm}$$
$$= 4t \text{ cm}^3$$
Density of leaf = 3 g per cm³
∴ 1 cm³ of leaf weighs 3 g
∴ $4t$ cm³ of leaf weighs $3 \times 4t$ g
∴ Mass of leaf = $12t$ g.

But you have found the mass of the leaf on the microbalance and you should now be able to calculate t. Give your answer as a fraction of a centimetre. How much smaller than this is an atom? We shall find out later.

Q. 4.17 Ten sheets of paper weigh 60 g. If each sheet measures 20 cm by 15 cm, what is the mass of
(a) one sheet,
(b) 1 cm² of paper,
(c) 1 mm² of paper.

Q. 4.18 A sheet of aluminium measures 10 cm by 10 cm and has mass 30 g. If the density of aluminium is taken as 3 g per cm³ what is the thickness of the sheet?

Q. 4.19 A sensitive balance gives a large deflection with a small mass. What would be the effect on the sensitivity of the microbalance of
(a) using a longer straw,
(b) putting the needle higher in the straw?

Trampoline. Demonstration in the gymnasium at the National Recreation Centre, Crystal Palace, London

5 Levers and springs

The laws of physics

Why? How? These are the two questions which physicists are always asking as they try to satisfy their curiosity and wonder about the world around us.

'Why' questions are difficult to answer. Why does an apple fall? Sir Isaac Newton, Fig. 5.1, said that it was due to the attraction of the earth, but is this a completely satisfactory explanation? Why does the earth attract it? The question has only been partly answered and you will find that this often happens with 'why' questions. Sometimes we have to accept that we can 'explain' no further and that the 'explanation' given is, for the present at any rate, the best possible.

'How' questions are easier to tackle. How does an apple fall? By this we may mean does it fall faster and faster or does it reach

Fig. 5.1

a certain speed and then continue to move with this speed? These are questions which ask for a description and can be satisfactorily answered by experiments.

You will have perhaps realized from the experiments you have done so far that the making of observations and possibly measurements are two important aspects of any scientific investigation. The next stage is the most difficult and involves looking to see if the results fall into any kind of simple pattern. The question is asked, 'Is there a connexion between the quantities investigated?' If such a relationship covering all cases can be found, it is stated as a rule or a principle or a law which then becomes, and this is most important, a powerful tool for predicting results.

Physics makes progress because physicists have faith in their belief that simple laws can be found. The work in this chapter will give you a real opportunity to discover for yourself some of these simple laws.

Investigating see-saws

A see-saw is usually a wooden plank balanced at its mid-point. It is an example of what physicists call a *lever*.

Experiment 5.1. Looking for a law of levers
The lever is shown in Fig. 5.2. Balance it with the central groove resting on the wedge. If it does not balance, stick some Plasticine below it at an appropriate point. Place one 'square penny' on each side and balance the lever. It will help if you:
A Put the pennies at the marks on the lever so that they are one, two or three, etc., divisions out from the centre and not three and a bit.

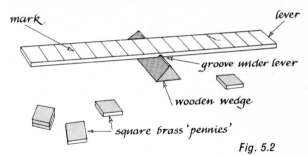

Fig. 5.2

B Think about the most accurate way of placing pennies on the lever. Would it be best to set them on the marks squarely, diagonally or how?
C Do the balancing so that the lever *just* tips over to one side when it is balanced. It will stay there and you will probably not manage to get it to balance exactly and remain level.

Number of pennies on left-hand side							Divisions from centre	Number of pennies on right-hand side						
7	6	5	4	3	2	1		1	2	3	4	5	6	7

Once the lever is balanced with two pennies, use other loads and distances. Make a table in your notebook like the one shown and record the various balancing arrangements. Can you find a rule or law which is always true when the lever is balanced?

Experiment 5.2. Games with a lever
Once you have found a rule you can use it to play these games with someone else.
A One person arranges several square pennies at marks on one side of the lever. His opponent

has then to find where to place *two* pennies to balance the lever.

B This game is called *Sym.* One person arranges several pennies on marks so that the lever is balanced. His opponent sketches the arrangement, removes the pennies and then has to get back to that arrangement in the *smallest number of moves.* In one move only two pennies can be placed or moved about on the lever and before and after each move the lever must be balanced.

Fig. 5.3

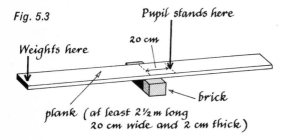

Pupil stands here

20 cm

Weights here

A

brick

plank (at least 2½ m long 20 cm wide and 2 cm thick)

Experiment 5.3. Weighing yourself roughly, using a see-saw

Balance a plank on a brick. Pupil *A* stands on the plank 20 cm from the brick whilst pupil *B* places kilogramme weights at the other end of the plank until it balances, Fig. 5.3. Work out what pupil *A* weighs.

Balancing problems

Q. 5.1 The four levers in Fig. 5.4 are pivoted at their mid-points and are loaded as shown. State whether each one is 'balanced' or 'unbalanced'. If it is unbalanced, say which end, right-hand or left-hand, tips downwards.

Q. 5.2 A girl weighing 30 kg sits at a distance of 2 m from the pivot (also called the fulcrum) of a see-saw. Where must a boy weighing 40 kg sit to balance the see-saw?

Q. 5.3 (*a*) In an experiment to weigh a boy a 6 m long plank is pivoted at its centre. The boy stands on the plank 40 cm from the pivot and is balanced by a load of 8 kg at the other end of the plank. What does he weigh?

(*b*) Can you think of another way of doing Experiment 5.3 using either a smaller load or a shorter plank? Does Fig. 5.5 give a clue?

Q. 5.4 (*a*) A plank has weight, but if it is pivoted so that it balances, it does not fall. We can therefore *imagine* that the whole weight of the plank acts downwards through the balancing point even though we know it is distributed all over. For a plank of the same thickness all along its length the balancing point is in the middle, Fig. 5.6*a*. Copy Fig. 5.6*a* and insert one arrow to

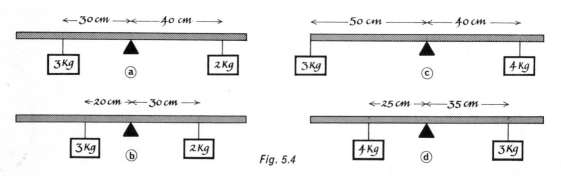

Fig. 5.4

Fig. 5.5

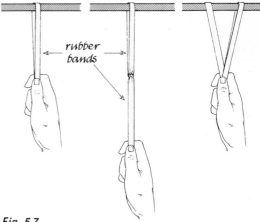

rubber bands

Fig. 5.7

show the weight of the plank and another for the upward push which the pivot must exert on the plank.

(b) In Fig. 5.6b a boy weighing 45 kg is shown standing on the end of an 8 m long heavy plank. Copy the diagram and insert an arrow to show where the weight of the plank acts. If the boy finds that when he is 1 m from the pivot the plank is just balanced, what does the plank weigh?

Stretching materials

Materials which are easily stretched, compressed or twisted and return to their previous shape when released are said to be *elastic*.

Experiment 5.4 Stretching and compressing materials

Stretch, compress, twist and bend a variety of materials including a latex foam block, a plastic foam block, a soft eraser, a wide steel spring, a rubber tube. Observe their behaviour.

Also try stretching rubber bands as shown in Fig. 5.7.

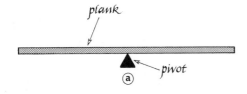

plank

pivot

(a)

Fig. 5.6

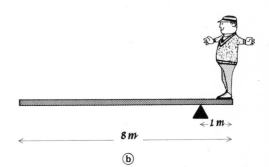

←1 m→

8 m

(b)

Experiment 5.5. Stretching a copper wire

Cut a 1 metre length of bare copper wire (SWG 32) from a *fresh* reel. (Old wire or wire with kinks must not be used.) Fasten each end to a pencil using short lengths of valve rubber to prevent the wire slipping, as in Fig. 5.8. Hold one pencil on the floor between the feet and the other with both hands.

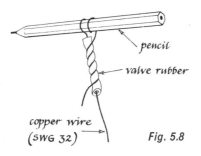

pencil

valve rubber

copper wire
(SWG 32)   *Fig. 5.8*

Gently pull the wire and feel it stretching. Pull more strongly and something surprising happens. How would you describe the feeling? Continue pulling until the wire breaks. Examine the broken ends with a magnifying glass or a microscope. How are they shaped?

Q. 5.5 Elastic materials have many uses. Can you explain how they are being used in Fig. 5.9 and on p. 51?

Atoms and elasticity

Can we form a picture which helps us to understand what is happening to the atoms in a wire when it is stretched? Metals, like most solids, are made up of many small crystals composed of atoms, spaced a little apart, in a regular pattern.

We learned earlier (p. 46) that scientists imagine atoms are held in position by strong, invisible forces which only act over short distances. One force causes an atom to attract its neighbours but another causes it to push them away, i.e. repel them. Normally a state of balance exists, with the attractive and repelling forces cancelling out so that a particular atom in a solid occupies more or less the same position.

If a metal rod is squeezed, the repelling force between the atoms increases more than the attractive one, and further squeezing becomes difficult. On the other hand, if a wire or rod is stretched the attractive effect increases and the wire resists. When the stretching force is removed, provided it is not too great, we picture the atoms recovering their original positions and the wire or rod its previous length. If too great a force is used, however, layers of atoms start sliding over one another, probably where a

Fig. 5.9

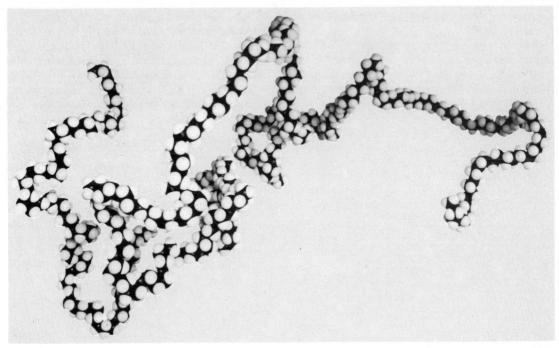

Fig. 5.10

metal crystal is not perfect and the wire thins and finally breaks. A crystal model of polystyrene balls such as we used in Demonstration 2.6*A* can be used to demonstrate layers of atoms slipping over one another.

Rubber can be stretched to several times its normal length. This is because a rubber molecule is very long (about 1/400 mm) and thin and in a piece of rubber lots of molecules are intertwined —like cooked spaghetti. When a stretching force is applied the molecules tend to straighten out and then coil up again when the force is removed. A model of a rubber molecule is shown in Fig. 5.10.

Q. 5.6 Mr Y. Howe is having further trouble with atoms. He says that he cannot connect the various effects you get when you stretch a wire until it breaks, as in Experiment 5.5, with what is happening to the atoms. Write a few sentences explaining the connexion to him.

Investigating springs

It is not easy to make measurements on the stretching of wires with simple apparatus. Can you suggest why? But we can look into the stretching of springs.

Experiment 5.6. Stretching a home-made copper spring

Cut about 1 m of bare copper wire (SWG 26) from a *fresh* reel. (Old wire or wire with kinks must not be used.) Make a spring by winding it round a pencil twenty-five to thirty times, Fig. 5.11a. Form a *twisted* loop at each end.

Fig. 5.11

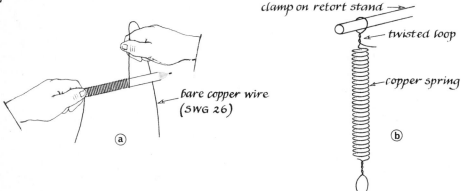
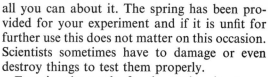

Hang the spring by one loop from a clamp in a retort-stand, Fig. 5.11b. Stretch the spring by adding a 10 g weight and measure the increase of length using a metre rule suitably supported. Add further 10 g weights and record all measurements in your notebook.

Investigate the behaviour of a copper spring made by winding 1 m of new copper wire on a knitting needle or something thin. Also try one wound on a test-tube.

Experiment 5.7. Stretching a steel spring

Repeat the previous experiment with a better spring, one made of steel wire which has loops at both ends and is ready to use. (See Appendix 5, p. 110.) Load it with 100 g weights and find out all you can about it. The spring has been provided for your experiment and if it is unfit for further use this does not matter on this occasion. Scientists sometimes have to damage or even destroy things to test them properly.

Examine the results for the steel spring to see if you can find any simple rule which tells how springs behave when they are stretched. For example, what happens when the load is doubled, or trebled and so on? Try to put your conclusion into words.

Graphs

Scientists find that it is often easier to discover laws from their results by drawing a graph. You can do this for the steel spring experiment by plotting your readings on a sheet of graph-paper Fig. 5.12.

To do this mark off the LOAD readings along OA (called the x-axis) and the STRETCH readings along OB (called the y-axis). Every pair of measurements will give a point such as P. Mark

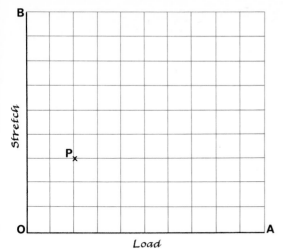

Fig. 5.12

the points with small crosses and draw a smooth line (a graph) passing through, or close to, all the points. How does the graph show up the simple law for springs? Does the law work even for the largest loads?

We sometimes find that our simple laws do not apply under all conditions. This is not because matter is misbehaving or because the law *we* have made has gone wrong but simply that the law has limitations. It is of course important to know what these are.

Draw a LOAD-STRETCH graph using the results from the copper spring experiment. Does the simple rule apply? If it does, has it any limitations?

Questions on springs

Q. 5.7 The bottom of a slightly stretched spring is opposite the zero mark on a scale when no load is attached to it. With a load of 200 g the bottom is pulled down to the 4 mark. What will the reading be for a load of (*a*) 100 g, (*b*) 300 g, (*c*) 150 g?

Q. 5.8 A vertical spring the coils of which are separate is 5 cm long when unloaded. With a load of 30 g it stretches to 8 cm.
(*a*) What length will it be when a load of 50 g hangs from it?
(*b*) If the length of the spring is 11 cm what load is carried?

Q. 5.9 Spring *A* is exactly the same as spring *B* but *A* is twice as long as *B*. A load of 1 kg stretches *A* by 1 cm. How much will 1 kg stretch *B*?

Q. 5.10 *X* and *Y* are two identical springs. A load of 10 g is attached to each one and both stretch 2 cm.
(*a*) If the springs are now arranged as in Fig. 5.13*a* with the bottom of *Y* opposite the zero on the scale, what will the reading be when 10 g is attached?
(*b*) If *X* and *Y* are next arranged as in Fig. 5.13*b*, what load will be required to stretch both springs by 2 cm?

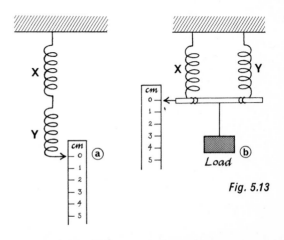

Fig. 5.13

Q. 5.11 The law connecting LOAD and STRETCH which you probably discovered when experimenting with springs is called Hooke's law. Write it out in your own words.

Q. 5.12 Name two devices which use strong springs and two which use weak springs.

Part of a complete experimental bathroom made by vacuum moulding two large sheets of 'Perspex'. Note the bath in the wall

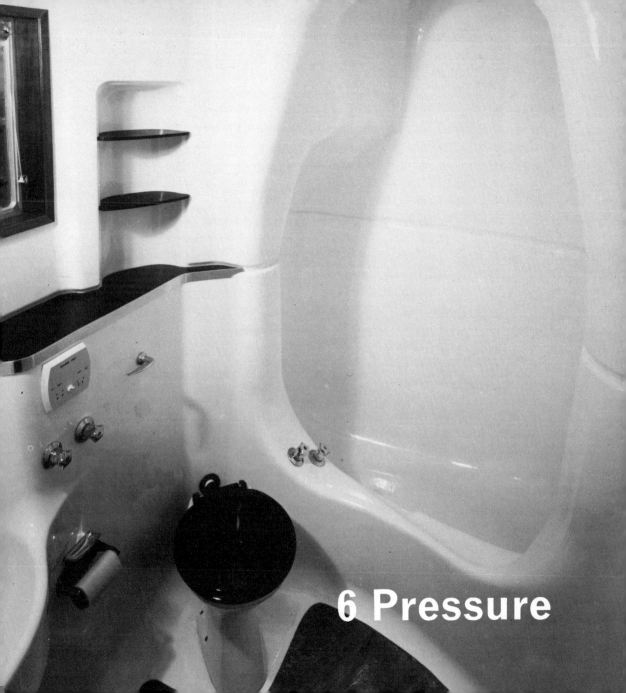

6 Pressure

CHAPTER SIX **PRESSURE**

Pressing problems

Problem 1 If you have ever tried to break a walnut in your hand without using nut-crackers you will know that it is almost impossible. However, by taking *two* nuts and squeezing them together it can be done, Fig. 6.1*a*. What is the explanation of this rather surprising effect?

Fig. 6.1a   *walnuts*

Problem 2 Suppose you had to rescue quickly someone who had fallen through the ice in a pond, Fig. 6.1*b*. If you had no other means of getting help to him would you walk across the ice or crawl? Walking would be quicker but would it be as safe as crawling?

Fig. 6.1b

Meaning of pressure

Consider Problem 2 first, since it is more urgent. You have probably decided that the wiser course of action would be to crawl. Let us see why.

If you walk, your weight will be mostly on one foot at any one time and if we suppose your foot is a rectangle (to make things easier) measuring 20 cm by 10 cm, Fig. 6.2a, then its area is 20 cm $\times$ 10 cm = 20 $\times$ 10 cm² = 200 cm². So we can say:

> *When walking:* your weight is spread over an area of 200 cm² of ice.

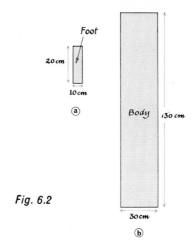

If you lie flat on your stomach when crawling and we assume that your body has the shape and measurements of Fig. 6.2b, then its area is 130 cm $\times$ 30 cm = 3900 cm². This is nearly 4000 cm² and so we can say:

> *When crawling:* your weight is spread over an area of about 4000 cm² of ice.

Fig. 6.2

We therefore see that although the *force* pressing on the ice due to your weight is the *same* in both cases, when you crawl the force is spread over a greater area of ice. In fact the area is twenty times greater (4000/200 = 40/2 = 20). This means that the force acting on each square centimetre of ice will be smaller than when walking. Can you say how many times smaller? The *force acting on unit area* (here 1 cm²) of a surface is called the *pressure* on that surface. In this example then the pressure exerted on the ice when crawling is twenty times less than when the same person walks. Therefore, if it is the pressure (and experience suggests it is) and not just the force which decides when the ice is going

to break, then crawling is clearly a less risky way of making the rescue.

There are many other effects that only make sense if we take into account the area of the surface on which a force acts as well as its size. In these cases the idea of pressure is a very useful one.

Experiment 6.1. Pressure effects

Find what load you can support with a meat hook balanced on the tip of your forefinger, Fig. 6.3, if the end of the hook is (a) blunt, (b) pointed —but take care. Explain the result.

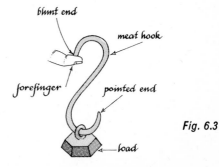

Fig. 6.3

Demonstration 6.2. Pressure box

Fig. 6.4a

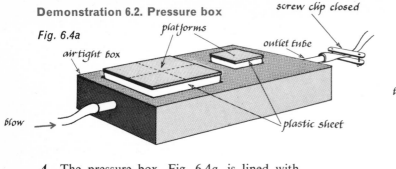

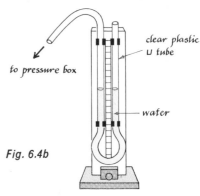

Fig. 6.4b

A The pressure box, Fig. 6.4*a*, is lined with plastic sheet and has two movable platforms, one four times the area of the other. Place a $\frac{1}{2}$ kg load on each platform and blow into the tube. Which platform rises first and why? Repeat with two, three, four and five $\frac{1}{2}$ kg loads on the large platform but still only one on the small one. When should both platforms rise together?

B If a U-tube half-full of water is connected to the outlet tube on the box, Fig. 6.4*b*, the effect of different pressures on the heights of water in the two arms can be seen. This provides us with a very simple means of measuring the pressure

Fig. 6.5a

Fig. 6.5b

Fig. 6.6

exerted by a gas—in this case by the air in the pressure box. Would you agree that the *difference* between the water levels in the U-tube roughly doubles when the pressure in the box doubles (as indicated by the load on the large platform)? Presently we shall take a closer look at this type of pressure gauge, called a U-tube manometer.

Q. 6.1 Use the idea of pressure to explain
(*a*) What advantage camels have with their large, flat feet, Fig. 6.5*a*.
(*b*) How wide caterpillar tracks help a bulldozer to move over soft ground, Fig. 6.5*b*.

Q. 6.2 Why should skis have a large area, Fig. 6.6?

Q. 6.3 Why is a girl in stiletto heels more likely to cause damage to a wooden floor than an elephant is?

Q. 6.4 Explain the walnut problem on page 62.

Liquid pressure

A solid presses downwards on the surface supporting it. We would expect a liquid, since it also has weight, to press down on the bottom of the vessel containing it and we know very well that if there is a hole in the bottom of a can of water the water is forced out. But does a liquid exert a pressure in any other direction?

Experiment 6.3 Investigating water pressure

A Using a hammer and a round nail make three or four holes in a tall can, all at the same level near the bottom but at different places, Fig. 6.7*a*. Fill the can with water and watch how the water spouts out into the sink or a bucket.

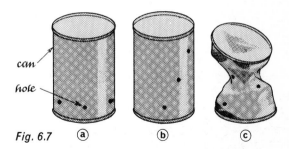

can

hole

Fig. 6.7   ⓐ   ⓑ   ⓒ

B Tape over all the holes except one and make another two—one near the top and one near the middle, but not quite one above the other, Fig. 6.7*b*. Try to have all the holes the same size. Fill the can with water and again observe how the water comes out. So far as possible keep the water at the same level in the can by pouring some in and see how much you collect from each hole in a certain time. Tape over the other two holes not required.
C Hammer the can so that it is partly crushed as in Fig. 6.7*c*. Make three holes near the bottom

on parts of the surface that are facing in different directions. Fill the can with water and note the direction in which the water spouts out from each hole.

The last part of Experiment 6.3 can also be done by half-filling a small polythene bag with water, gripping it tightly round the neck and making a few pin-holes in different parts of the bag, Fig. 6.8.

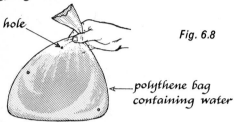

hole

Fig. 6.8

—polythene bag
containing water

What conclusions have you reached about (*a*) the direction(s) in which a liquid exerts a pressure and (*b*) the effect of the depth of liquid on the value of the pressure exerted at that depth?

Q. 6.5 Explain why (*a*) the wall of a reservoir must be thicker at the bottom than at the top, Fig. 6.9, and (*b*) why submarines, divers and common fish cannot descend beyond a certain depth?

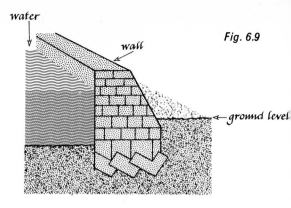

water

Fig. 6.9

wall

←—ground level

A liquid finds its own level

This is a saying you may have heard before. A few demonstrations will show what it means and knowing about liquid pressure should help you to explain why liquids behave in this way.

Demonstration 6.4. Water levels

A Arrange a piece of clear plastic tubing as in Fig. 6.10*a* with the clip closed and different heights of water in each arm of the U. How does the pressure at *L* due to the water above it compare with that at *M*? Open the clip: what happens? How do the pressures at *L* and *M* now compare?

Fig. 6.10

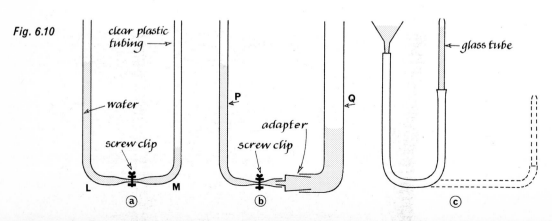

clear plastic
tubing —→

—water

screw clip

L   M

(a)

P

adapter
screw clip

(b)

Q

←—glass tube

(c)

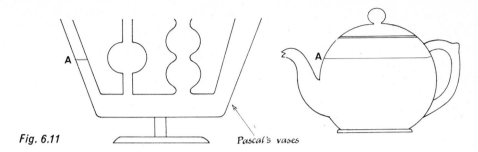

Fig. 6.11   Pascal's vases

B Set up the apparatus shown in Fig. 6.10*b*. Open the clip. The levels should settle to be the same on both sides. This may seem strange for there is a greater weight of water in *Q* than in *P* but the weight in *Q* is spread over a greater area since it is in a wider tube. What can you say about the pressure at the bottom of *P* compared with that at the bottom of *Q* when the levels are the same? Can you complete this statement: 'The pressure at the bottom of a column of water does not depend on the width of the column but only on the ...... of the column.'

C Fill the apparatus of Fig. 6.10*c* with water and observe the height of the water jet when the glass tube is held below the level of water in the funnel. Does the jet find its own level, i.e. the level of water in the funnel? If not, why not?

Q. 6.6 If liquid is poured into the vessels in Fig. 6.11 until it reaches level *A* in the parts shown, where would the levels be in the other parts?

Q. 6.7 Explain in terms of liquid pressure why a liquid tries to find its own level.

Q. 6.8 A knowledge of liquid pressure is essential to the engineers who are responsible for our water-supply. Fig. 6.12 shows part of the Pont du Gard, near Nîmes in France. It is about two thousand years old and was built by the Romans as an aqueduct to carry water from a source 40 kilometres away. But do you think that it was really necessary to make such a grand structure to carry water across a valley? How do we manage this nowadays?

Fig. 6.12

Atmospheric pressure

Air is not very dense, as we discovered in Demonstration 4.4, but if there is a lot of it, its weight is considerable. We live at the bottom of a vast sea of air, called the atmosphere, which stretches upwards for many kilometres. The atmosphere exerts a pressure which at sea level is fairly large as we shall see in the next three demonstrations.

Demonstration 6.5. Collapsing a can

Fit a large empty syrup-tin (from the school kitchen) or an oil-tin which has been cleaned out, with a rubber stopper having a short length of glass or metal tubing through it. Connect it to a vacuum pump with pressure tubing, Fig. 6.13, and slowly remove the air. Explain what happens. In what direction(s) does atmospheric pressure act? (A plastic bottle can also be used for this experiment.)

How could the tin be returned more or less to its original shape?

Demonstration 6.6. Blowing up a balloon

Place a partly blown up balloon in a bell-jar or other strong glass vessel from which the air can be removed by a vacuum pump, Fig. 6.14.

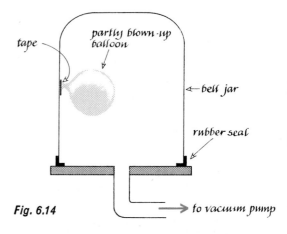

Fig. 6.14

Account for the behaviour of the balloon as the air is taken out. Is there any evidence to suggest that the air inside the balloon pushes equally in all directions?

Demonstration 6.7. The obedient hole

Knock a hole with a hammer and nail in the bottom of a can with a tight-fitting lid. Also make a hole in the lid. Fill the can by immersing it under water, replace the lid, put your forefinger over the hole in the lid and remove the can from the water. You can then cause the

Fig. 6.13

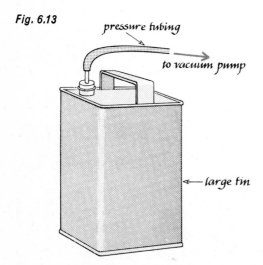

water to escape from the lower hole simply by easing your finger off the hole in the lid, Fig. 6.15.

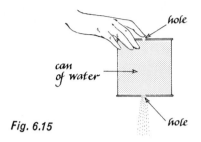

Fig. 6.15

What keeps the water in when the hole in the lid is covered and why does it come out when it is uncovered?

It is interesting to investigate what happens when the lower hole in the can is made larger and larger.

About 1650 Otto von Guericke, the Mayor of Magdeburg, performed a striking experiment in the presence of the Emperor of Germany. Having invented the first vacuum pump, von Guericke used it to remove the air from two hollow copper hemispheres, about 30 cm across, fitted together

Fig. 6.16

to give an airtight sphere. So good was his pump that two teams, each of eight horses, were required to separate the hemispheres, Fig. 6.16. Why was such a great force necessary?

A similar experiment can be done using small model hemispheres or two moistened rubber suckers which are pushed together to expel most of the air, Fig. 6.17.

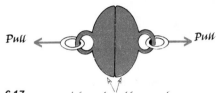

Fig. 6.17   moistened rubber suckers

Our demonstrations have shown that atmospheric pressure is substantial and acts not only downwards but, like a liquid, equally in all directions. It is only when we upset the balance of things by removing air from one place that the pressure of the air becomes noticeable. We do not normally feel air pressure ourselves, since it presses in all directions; furthermore, the pressure inside our bodies is the same as that outside.

Bourdon pressure gauge

This is one of the two devices we shall use to measure the pressure exerted by a fluid, i.e. by a liquid or a gas. It works rather like the blow-out toy which is popular at Christmas. The harder you blow into the paper tube, the more does it uncurl, Fig. 6.18a. In the Bourdon pressure

paper tube   (a)   **Fig. 6.18**

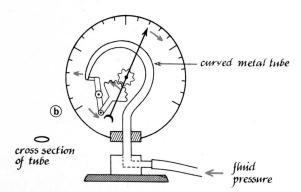

curved metal tube

(b)

cross section of tube

fluid pressure

gauge, Fig. 6.18b, when a fluid pressure is applied, the curved metal tube straightens itself out according to the pressure and rotates a pointer over a scale. The pressure can thus be read off directly. Car oil pressure gauges and the gauges on gas-cylinders, vacuum pumps and steam-boilers are of this type.

Demonstration 6.8. The Bourdon pressure gauge

Look at the pressure reading on the gauge. Can you suggest why the reading is not zero? Is there already a fluid pressure acting on the gauge?

Suck at the end of a piece of rubber or plastic tubing connected to the gauge. Account for what happens to the reading. Next blow into the gauge and explain what the new reading tells us.

U-tube manometer

This pressure gauge consists of a U-shaped tube of clear plastic or glass half-filled with a liquid, Fig. 6.19a. The liquid or gas the pressure of which is to be measured is connected to one side of the U-tube; the other side is usually open to the air.

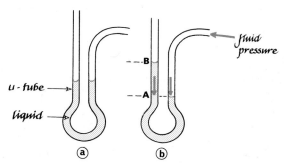

fluid pressure

u - tube

liquid

(a)   (b)

Fig. 6.19

Suppose a fluid pressure is applied to a manometer, for example, by blowing gently into it, and that the liquid levels settle as in Fig. 6.19b. The *difference AB* in the heights of the two columns is called the 'head' of liquid and is a measure of the pressure created by blowing. The greater the pressure the greater the difference. The fluid pressure applied to the right-hand tube of the manometer is supporting the column of liquid *AB* and therefore must be exerting the same pressure as the column of liquid does at *A*. Pressures measured by a manometer are usually stated as being so many centimetres of water or whatever liquid is used in the manometer.

Experiment 6.9. Measuring the gas pressure with a water manometer

A Half-fill a small manometer with water and connect it to the gas supply. Turn on the gas-tap and measure the difference of the water levels in centimetres.

B Now connect the gas supply to *P* and *Q* in turn, in the 'U-tube' manometer of Fig. 6.20. Is the difference of the water levels always the same as in *A*?

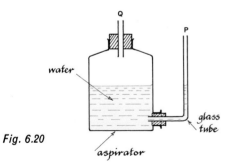

Fig. 6.20

Experiment 6.10. Measuring lung pressure with a water manometer

Attach to a $2\frac{1}{2}$ m water manometer a short length of glass tubing (with smooth ends) to act as a mouthpiece, Fig. 6.21. Blow into the manometer and get someone to measure your lung pressure in centimetres of water. Sterilize the mouthpiece in diluted TCP before anyone else uses it.

Experiment 6.11. Measuring lung pressure with a mercury manometer

Repeat the previous experiment using a 1 m mercury manometer and obtain your lung pressure in centimetres of mercury.

Compare this result with the one obtained using the water manometer. Roughly how many times greater is the one result than the other?

Hold a small screw-top plastic bottle (or a beaker) half-full of water in one hand, and a similar vessel half-full of mercury in the other. Mercury is clearly much denser than water. The density of water is 1 g per cm^3 and of mercury about 13·5 g per cm^3. Can you connect these facts with your results?

Q. 6.9 (*a*) Copy the following statement and fill in the two missing words: 'The pressure due to a column of liquid depends on the . . . . . . of the column and the . . . . of the liquid.'

(*b*) For what kinds of pressure measurement would a mercury manometer be preferable to a water one?

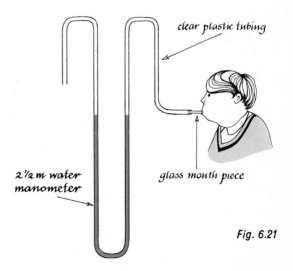

Fig. 6.21

Q. 6.10 If the manometer used to measure the pressure of the gas-supply had one limb three times as wide as the other, what would be the effect on the result? Give a reason for your answer.

Q. 6.11 When a water manometer is connected to a gas-supply the difference of levels is 4·5 scale divisions.
(a) What will the difference be with a mercury manometer if mercury is 13·5 times as dense as water? Give your answer as a fraction of a scale division.
(b) With an oil manometer the difference is 5·5 divisions. Compare the densities of the oil and water.

Mercury barometer

Atmospheric pressure changes from one place to another and from day to day. It can be measured by a kind of manometer called a mercury barometer.

The U-tube manometer really measures the *difference* between the pressures on the liquid surfaces in each tube. For example, in Fig. 6.22a each surface is acted on equally by atmospheric pressure and the levels are the same. In Fig. 6.22b the manometer shows that the gas pressure

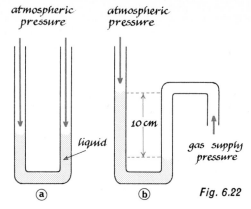

atmospheric pressure   *atmospheric pressure*

liquid

10 cm

gas supply pressure

(a)   (b)   *Fig. 6.22*

is 10 cm of water *greater* than atmospheric pressure and this is what we mean when we say that the gas pressure is 10 cm of water.

A U-tube manometer can be used to measure atmospheric pressure if we remove the air completely from one tube so that atmospheric pressure only acts in the other. The manometer will then measure the difference between atmospheric pressure and the zero pressure of a vacuum.

Demonstration 6.12. Measuring atmospheric pressure with a U-tube mercury manometer
Connect one side of a 1 m U-tube manometer to a vacuum pump as shown in Fig. 6.23. The flask

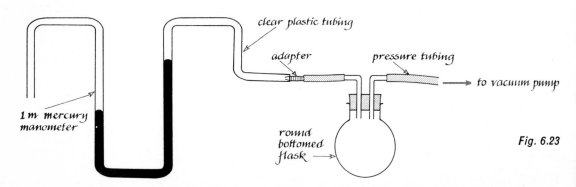

clear plastic tubing

adapter   *pressure tubing*

to vacuum pump

1 m mercury manometer

round bottomed flask

Fig. 6.23

acts as trap between the tube and the pump to ensure mercury does not enter the pump. Remove the air *slowly* (the flask assists this) and observe the mercury levels. After a time they remain steady even with the pump still working. What conclusion may be drawn? Measure the atmospheric pressure in centimetres of mercury.

Is it necessary to have a U-tube?

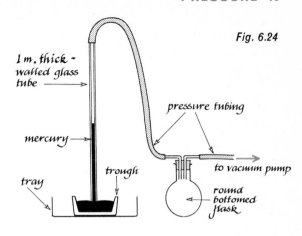

Fig. 6.24

1 m. thick-walled glass tube

mercury

tray

trough

pressure tubing

to vacuum pump

round bottomed flask

Demonstration 6.13. Measuring atmospheric pressure with a straight tube

Set up a 1 m thick-walled glass tube vertically with its lower end in a trough of mercury set in a tray. Connect the top of the tube (via a trap) to the vacuum pump with pressure tubing, Fig. 6.24. After pumping measure the height of the mercury above that in the trough. If the space in the tube above the mercury is not a vacuum what difference will this make to the value obtained for atmospheric pressure?

It is possible to create the vacuum without a pump.

Demonstration 6.14. Making a simple barometer

Using a small funnel pour mercury into a thick-walled glass tube, about a metre long and closed at one end, until it is full to within 1 cm of the open end, Fig. 6.25a. Place your thumb over the

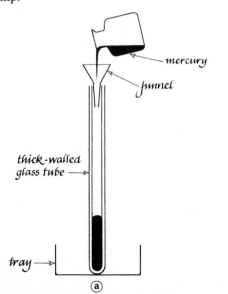

mercury

funnel

thick-walled glass tube

tray

(a)

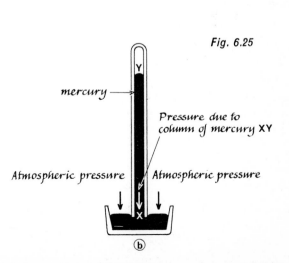

Fig. 6.25

mercury

Y

Pressure due to column of mercury XY

Atmospheric pressure

Atmospheric pressure

X

(b)

open end, tilt the tube so that the 1 cm air bubble rises *slowly* up the tube to the closed end and collects on the way small air bubbles trapped in the mercury. Reinvert the tube to bring the large air bubble back to the open end. Repeat this process a few times and then fill the tube to the top with mercury.

Place the thumb on the open end again and invert the tube into a trough of mercury. Observe what happens when the thumb is removed; clamp the tube. We have made a simple mercury barometer. The atmospheric pressure balances the pressure at X due to the weight of the column of mercury XY, Fig. 6.25b. XY therefore gives the atmospheric pressure in centimetres of mercury.

The space at the top of the mercury contains no air; it is a vacuum. How could we test this?

Would it make any difference if the tube was wider?

Roughly how long would the tube have to be if water was used instead of mercury?

A few refinements convert a simple mercury barometer into the accurate type of barometer, used by scientists and meteorologists, called the Fortin barometer.

Weather forecasts

Measurements of atmospheric pressure at recording stations all over Western Europe and at weather ships in the Atlantic help meteorologists to forecast the weather. At a central office a map like that in Fig. 6.26 is built up from all the readings.

On this weather map lines, called isobars, are drawn joining places of equal atmospheric pressure (the coloured lines in Fig. 6.26). If they

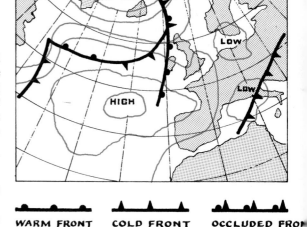

TYPICAL ATLANTIC WEATHER MAP

WARM FRONT   COLD FRONT   OCCLUDED FRONT

Fig. 6.26

enclose a region of high pressure the system is called an *anticyclone*. Anticyclones are generally accompanied by clear skies with long sunny days in summer; in winter there is the possibility of frost and perhaps fog. Once an anticyclone has formed it often does not move for several days and covers a wide area. In Britain the average number of anticyclones per month is seven, September having the highest average with ten, July and August having the least with five!

A *depression* or cyclone is associated with a region of low pressure and these are a common feature of British weather. They form in the North Atlantic, are a few hundred kilometres in width and travel at about 30 km/h near the British Isles. Each one lasts for a few days and they usually bring widespread rain. Strong south-westerly winds often occur as well.

Within a depression there are warm and cold fronts. A warm front marks the line of advancing warm air and a cold one indicates advancing cold air. Eventually the cold front overtakes the warm front and the single front which results is called an occluded front. At this stage the depression dies away. Various fronts are shown on Fig. 6.26.

Winds arise from differences in pressure and the greater these are (i.e. isobars close together) the stronger the winds. We might expect the wind to blow directly from places of high pressure to those of low pressure across the isobars. However the rotation of the earth disturbs things and they tend to blow along the isobars, clockwise round an anticyclone and anticlockwise round a depression in the northern hemisphere.

Besides pressure readings, meteorological stations also record temperature, wind speed, humidity, cloud cover, etc.

You should study the weather map published daily in one of the national newspapers.

Some questions

Q. 6.12 (*a*) Is the reading of a barometer tube affected if the tube is tilted?

(*b*) Does the width of a barometer tube make any difference to the reading? Can you suggest why?

(*c*) How would you find out if there was any air at the top of a barometer tube without the help of another barometer? How would the pressure of any such air affect the reading?

(*d*) When making a simple barometer the tube is inverted so that the large air bubble rises up the tube and collects any small ones in the mercury on the way. Why does the large air bubble rise in this way?

Q. 6.13 A mercury barometer is shown in Fig. 6.27. The vessel is open to the atmosphere through tube *S*.

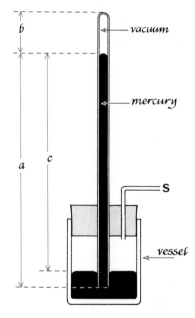

Fig. 6.27

(*a*) Which height, *a*, *b* or *c* gives atmospheric pressure?

(*b*) What happens when *S* is connected to a vacuum pump?

(*c*) If the vacuum pump is disconnected and replaced by a bicycle pump (connected through a suitable valve) what happens when the pump is operated?

Q. 6.14 Three thick glass tubes *A*, *B* and *C*, of lengths 70 cm, 90 cm and 110 cm, all closed at one end, are completely filled with mercury so as to exclude all air bubbles and then inverted in a vessel of mercury as in Fig. 6.28. The atmospheric pressure is 75 cm of mercury.

Fig. 6.28

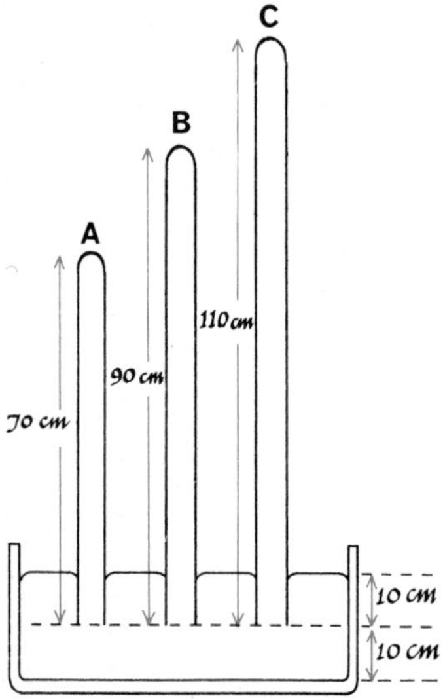

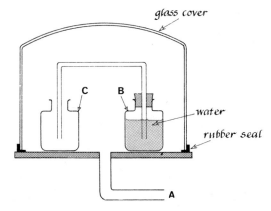

(a) Copy the diagram and show what happens to the mercury in each tube. Mark distances.

(b) Tube *B* is pushed 5 cm farther down into the vessel. What happens to the mercury level in the tube?

(c) What happens if tube *C* is raised 5 cm out of the vessel?

Q. 6.15 (a) Atmospheric pressure equals the pressure due to a column of mercury about 80 cm high. How high would an 'atmosphere' of mercury be if it exerted the same pressure as the actual atmosphere?

(b) If we take mercury as being 13·5 times as dense as water, how high would an 'atmosphere' of water be? Give your answer in metres.

(c) How deep would a lake be for the pressure at the bottom to be twice the value of the atmospheric pressure given in (a)?

Q. 6.16 You have been telling Mr Y. Howe about barometers and atmospheric pressure but he says he finds it hard to believe that atmospheric pressure can support a column of water about 10 m high. Describe an experiment which you could perform to convince him, using a vacuum pump, a 12 m length of thick-walled, clear plastic tubing and a bucket of water.

Q. 6.17 (a) In Fig. 6.29, when tube *A* is connected to a vacuum pump, water passes from bottle *B*, which is closed by a stopper, to bottle *C* which is open. Why?

(b) What will happen when the pump is stopped and air allowed to enter the glass cover?

Fig. 6.29

Aneroid barometer

A mercury barometer, although accurate, is bulky and not easily moved. The aneroid (meaning 'not wet') barometer is portable and more convenient.

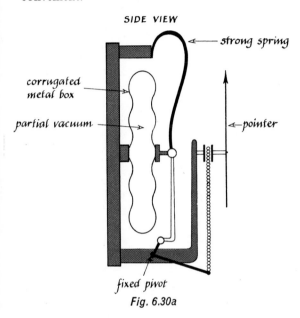

SIDE VIEW

strong spring

corrugated metal box

partial vacuum

pointer

fixed pivot

Fig. 6.30a

It consists of a partially evacuated, thin metal box, with corrugated sides to increase its strength, Fig. 6.30a. The box is prevented from collapsing by a strong spring. If the atmospheric pressure increases the centre of the box moves in, if it decreases the spring pulls the centre out. A system of levers magnifies this movement and the last lever is attached to a chain which causes a pointer to move over a scale marked in centimetres of mercury, Fig. 6.30b. Low pressures are recorded when water vapour, which is less dense than air, replaces air and this suggests rain is likely.

A sensitive aneroid barometer can be used as an altimeter in aircraft since atmospheric pressure decreases as the height above sea-level increases. It is marked in metres instead of centimetres of mercury and is set to zero before the plane takes off so that the pilot will know his

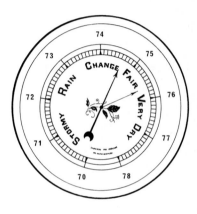

Fig. 6.30b

height above the runway. If the destination airport is 1000 m above the level of the take-off one the altimeter must again be adjusted before landing, otherwise it will read 1000 m when the aircraft is at ground-level.

Using air pressure

Air pressure can be made to help us if we create a pressure difference by either reducing or increasing the air pressure at one place so that it is different from the normal value.

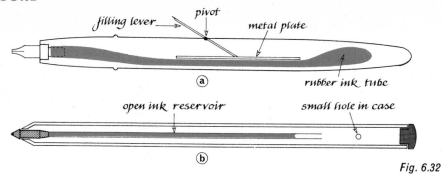

Fig. 6.32

Q. 6.18. Drinking straw When you drink milk or lemonade through a straw you may think that you are 'pulling' the liquid up the straw. However, you are merely removing some of the air in the straw thus lowering the pressure inside it. Atmospheric pressure pushing down on the surface of the liquid in the bottle, now being greater than the air pressure inside the straw, thus forces liquid up the straw, Fig. 6.31a. In Fig. 6.31b a glass tube passes through a good-fitting rubber stopper in a bottle of liquid. Do you think you would get a drink with this arrangement?

Q. 6.19. Fountain-pen In Fig. 6.32a the parts of a fountain-pen are shown. Explain how this kind of pen relies on air pressure for filling. Such a pen would leak in a high-flying aircraft. Why? The ball-point pen was invented to overcome this difficulty. Examine Fig. 6.32b or a ball-point pen if you have one available and explain how the problem has been solved.

Q. 6.20. Vacuum cleaner A vacuum cleaner is shown in Fig. 6.33. How does it pick up dust?

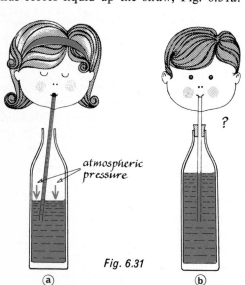

Fig. 6.31

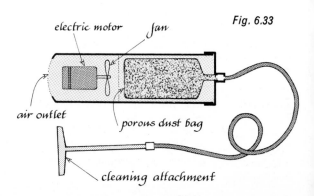

Fig. 6.33

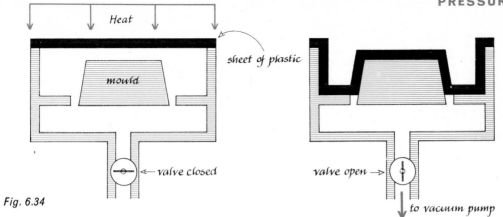

Heat

sheet of plastic

mould

valve closed

valve open →

to vacuum pump

Fig. 6.34

Q. 6.21. Moulding plastics Air pressure is used to form a sheet of plastic, previously softened by heating, into a complicated shape such as a basin. Work out from Fig. 6.34 how this happens. The picture on p. 61 shows part of a bathroom made by moulding two sheets of 'Perspex'.

Q. 6.22. Air brakes Some lorries have vacuum-assisted brakes and a notice on the back saying 'Caution—air brakes'. How do you think the brakes work and why is the notice necessary?

Q. 6.23. Compressed air Air which has been squeezed or compressed so that it exerts a greater pressure than normal has many uses. What is it being used to do in Figs. 6.35 and 6.36?

Fig. 6.36

Fig. 6.35

KILOMETRES

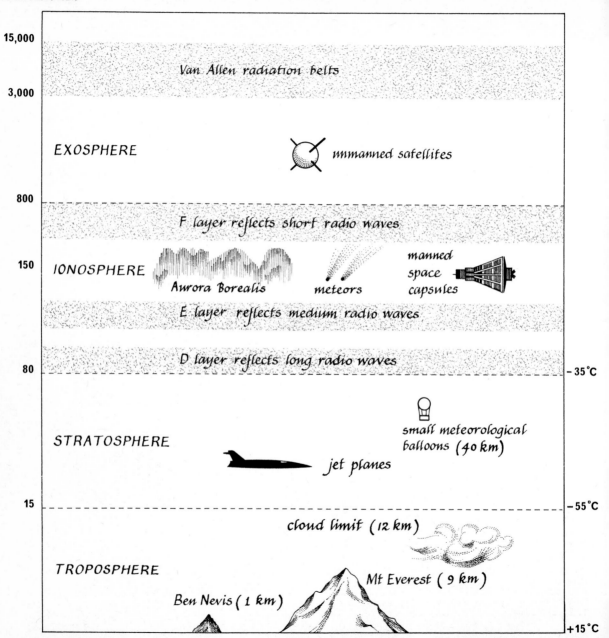

15,000

3,000

Van Allen radiation belts

EXOSPHERE — unmanned satellites

800

F layer reflects short radio waves

150

IONOSPHERE

Aurora Borealis   meteors   manned space capsules

E layer reflects medium radio waves

D layer reflects long radio waves

80 — −35°C

STRATOSPHERE

small meteorological balloons (40 km)

jet planes

15 — −55°C

cloud limit (12 km)

TROPOSPHERE

Mt Everest (9 km)

Ben Nevis (1 km)

+15°C

Fig. 6.37

The earth's atmosphere

If the atmosphere had the same density all the way up it can be shown that it would only need to be 8 km high to produce the pressure we experience at sea-level. Aircraft, however, whose engines require a supply of air, fly well above this height, and a great deal of other evidence from balloons, rockets and artificial satellites shows that it extends beyond 150 km. Its density becomes less and less the higher we rise and 50 per cent of its weight is below 6 km.

As well as providing us with the air we require for breathing, the atmosphere shields us from the intense heat of the sun by day, and by night it helps to keep the earth warm. It also absorbs

2. The *stratosphere* extends from 15 to 80 km and contains no water vapour and therefore no clouds. The temperature is low but nearly constant and winds always blow in the same direction. Conditions are almost ideal for flying.

3. The *ionosphere* stretches from 80 to about 800 km. It contains electrically charged particles (called ions) which reflect radio waves back to earth and, along with communication satellites, makes world-wide radio possible.

4. The *exosphere* is the part beyond 800 km where the Van Allen radiation belts exist, Fig. 6.38. These are two regions of dangerous atomic

Fig. 6.38

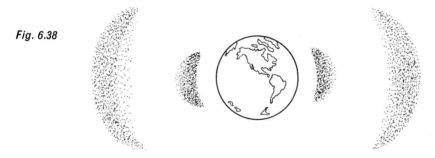

Van Allen radiation belts

X-rays and the harmful part of ultraviolet radiation, both emitted by the sun.

The four main regions of the earth's atmosphere are shown in Fig. 6.37.

1. The *troposphere* is the first 15 km or so. In it the temperature falls as we ascend and weather changes occur, i.e. clouds, rain, snow, etc. are formed.

particles, discovered from instruments in artificial satellites and lunar space probes, at distances of 3000 and 15,000 km from the earth.

Our bodies are designed to work under normal atmospheric pressure. At very low pressures, blood and water in the body would boil and it would be impossible to live. Modern high-flying

Fig. 6.39

aircraft have pressurized cabins in which the air pressure is increased sufficiently above that outside to safeguard the passengers.

An effect experienced by air passengers when changes of pressure occur is ear 'popping'. This is due to the air pressure in the middle section of the ear being different from that in the outer ear and distorting the ear-drum. Swallowing helps to equalize the pressures and 'unpops' the ears.

Astronauts must take their own atmospheres with them in their pressurized space suits, Fig. 6.39, and space capsules.

Model of part of the molecule of deoxyribonucleic acid (DNA) showing some of its millions of atoms. DNA plays a vital part in the chemistry of living things and is thought to carry the code which decides what we inherit from our parents. Its very complicated structure was unravelled using X-rays

7 Models and molecules

CHAPTER SEVEN **MODELS AND MOLE-CULES**

Model of a gas

You can often smell a meal being cooked even though you are not present in the kitchen. A gasworks, a brewery, a chemical factory and a farmyard have their own particular odours by which they may be identified. Such odours are caused by gases or vapours, given off at one place and travelling all around.

Scientists believe that the molecules of gases and vapours are always on the move, travelling very fast, filling all the space they can and bouncing off everything they meet. The pressure exerted by a gas in, for example, a balloon or a car tyre is considered to be due to the gas molecules continually bombarding the walls of their container. The next experiment may help you to think about gas molecules.

Experiment 7.1. Shaking marbles in a tray

Place two dozen marbles (about 15 mm diameter) in a tray (30 cm by 20 cm with 1 cm high vertical sides) having a sheet of cork

Fig. 7.1

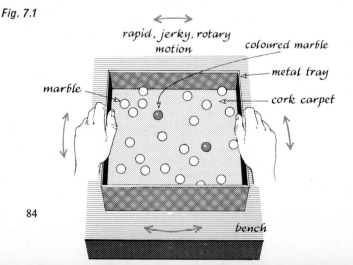

inside. Grip the *sides* of the tray and, with *the whole of the bottom* on the bench, keep it moving with a rapid, jerky, rotatory motion, Fig. 7.1.

A Concentrate first on one particular marble. Observe its progress. How would you describe the path it follows? Does it always have the same speed?
B The marbles have collisions. With what? Listen carefully to see if the sound of the collisions is always the same. If we think of the marbles as representing gas molecules, what indicates 'pressure' in the tray of moving marbles?

The tray with marbles dashing here and there is a *model* or imaginary picture of a gas. It certainly does not prove that gas molecules are little round balls in constant motion but it shows that a particles-in-motion explanation of some of the properties of gases could be true. Scientists often form such models to help them to think about things, such as molecules, which they cannot see directly.

Q. 7.1 (*a*) Why does the pressure in a bicycle tyre increase when more air is pumped into it?
(*b*) How would you demonstrate the effect using the marbles model?

Brownian motion

How can we find out if gas molecules really are dashing about all over the place? They are too small for us to see and they could also be travelling too fast. Suppose, however, that we had some tiny specks of, say, smoke-ash, floating in the air, just large enough to be seen with a microscope, what would happen to them? Would they be pushed around in a haphazard way by air molecules darting about and bouncing off them? We will first try to imitate the process with the tray of marbles.

Experiment 7.2. More tray shaking

Add one or two large marbles (25 mm diameter) to two dozen ordinary marbles in the tray. The large marbles represent visible smoke particles and the others invisible air molecules. Agitate the tray as before with a jerky, circular motion. The larger marbles are jostled by the smaller ones. How does their motion compare with that of the smaller marbles?

Will the effect be the same with real smoke particles and real molecules? Let us try.

Experiment 7.3. Observing smoke particles with a microscope

The apparatus consists of a horizontal lamp (usually a festoon lamp) and a glass rod to focus the light on the middle of a small glass cell, Fig. 7.2a. Remove the cover from the apparatus and

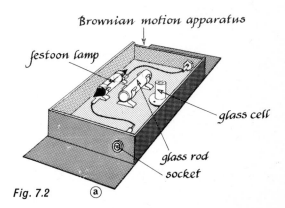

Brownian motion apparatus

festoon lamp

glass cell

glass rod

socket

Fig. 7.2   (a)

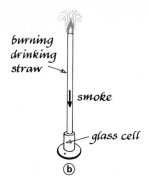

burning
drinking
straw

smoke

glass cell

7.2 contd.

(b)

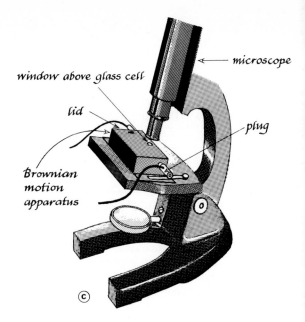

window above glass cell

microscope

lid

plug

Brownian
motion
apparatus

(c)

fill the glass cell with smoke. The easiest way to do this is to light the top end of a drinking straw and hold it upright so that smoke pours down inside the straw into the cell at the bottom, Fig. 7.2*b*. When it is full replace the cover *securely* on the apparatus and place it on the microscope platform, Fig. 7.2*c*.

Connect a 12 volt supply for the lamp to the terminals on the apparatus and carefully focus the microscope on the smoke cell until you can see the smoke particles as bright points of light. Observe them for a few minutes. Do they continually move jerkily through short distances in many directions? (Smoke specks which are not in focus will appear as round patches of light.)

It would now seem reasonable to conclude that although we cannot see air molecules themselves colliding we can see the results of their collisions with smoke particles. The effect, called *Brownian motion*, is also given by small particles suspended in a liquid and was first noticed by a Scottish botanist, Robert Brown, with pollen grains in water.

Q. 7.2 Mr Y. Howe is interested in the Brownian motion experiment with smoke particles and has some difficult questions to ask. Answer them as best you can.

(*a*) How do you know that the smoke particles are not behaving as they do because of vibration of the apparatus due to say traffic outside or because they have a light shining on them?

(*b*) What would happen if you used smoke particles which were (i) smaller but still visible, (ii) larger?

Diffusion

An effect known as *diffusion* provides further evidence, perhaps less spectacular than Brownian motion, for the view that molecules are always on the move.

Demonstration 7.4. Diffusion of nitrogen dioxide in air

Prepare some brown nitrogen dioxide gas by pouring a mixture of equal volumes of concentrated nitric acid and water on some copper turnings in the bottom of a gas-jar. When the action has stopped and the gas has had time to cool to room temperature, invert another gas-jar

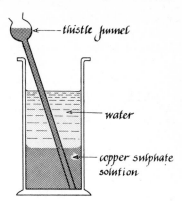

Fig. 7.4

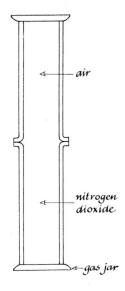

Fig. 7.3

of the jar, Fig. 7.4. There should be a distinct line of separation between the liquids and if too much disturbance is caused by removing the funnel, leave it in the jar.

After a few days the blue copper sulphate solution will have diffused into the water. Will the reverse have occurred? It seems that liquid molecules too move about.

Demonstration 7.6. Diffusion of potassium chromate in gelatine

Make enough jelly from gelatine and hot water (30 g gelatine to 500 cm³ of water is satisfactory) to fill one boiling tube and half-fill three others. Allow the jelly to set in the tubes. Completely fill the half-filled tubes with potassium chromate solution and insert a rubber stopper in each tube so as to exclude air bubbles.

Clamp the tubes so that one is upright, one inverted, one on its side and the one full of jelly is anyhow. Observe them after a day or so. Does diffusion occur in a jelly?

Replace the chromate solution in one of the tubes by clean water and again note the result after a day.

of air on top of it, Fig. 7.3. Place a white screen behind and observe. Can you explain what occurs in terms of molecules?

Demonstration 7.5. Diffusion of copper sulphate in water

Half-fill a gas-jar with water. *Slowly* pour a concentrated solution of copper sulphate down a long thistle funnel which reaches to the bottom

Demonstration 7.7. Diffusion of copper sulphate crystals in water

Drop some large copper sulphate crystals into a gas-jar full of water. Examine after a few days.

Q. 7.3 The air making up our atmosphere consists mainly of two gases, oxygen and nitrogen. Oxygen is slightly denser than nitrogen so we might expect two separate layers to be formed. This has not happened and the atmosphere is a mixture of the two. Explain this.

Q. 7.4 (*a*) Why does diffusion occur more quickly in a gas than in a liquid?

(*b*) Even in a gas diffusion is still quite a slow process. Why?

Kinetic theory

It is now time to review our knowledge of atoms and molecules. According to the picture we have built up, the differences between solids, liquids and gases arise from the *spacing* and the *motion* of their atoms or molecules.

1. Solid. In a solid we think of atoms or molecules arranged in a regular pattern, spaced a little apart, but close enough to exert strong forces on each other which hold them together tightly to form crystals. The strong forces are exerted only over short distances and are of two types—short-range attractions (pulls) and very short-range repulsions (pushes). Normally those acting on a particular atom balance (see p. 56) but if the atoms are pushed closer together by applying pressure they repel one another due to the repulsions becoming greater than the attractions. On the other hand if we pull them farther apart the attractive forces exceed the repulsions and the solid resists.

In addition we also imagine that in a solid the atoms and molecules are vibrating to and fro about their average position but not moving around.

2. Liquid. In liquids the molecules are still fairly close together but their motion is not restricted to vibration. They can move very quickly over short distances before they are repelled, as frequently happens, in a collision with another molecule. Attractive forces do exist between the molecules but they are smaller than in a solid and whereas a solid can support itself a liquid has to be contained in a vessel.

3. Gas. Molecules are imagined to be much farther apart in gases than in solids or liquids. The forces of attraction between them are now so small that they have almost complete freedom and dash around on their own in all the space available. When one does come very close to another molecule, a strong repulsive force is exerted and a collision occurs.

This model of the three states of matter is called the *kinetic theory*; kinetic means 'due to motion'. Here are two demonstrations which may help to illustrate the theory.

Demonstration 7.8. Two-dimensional kinetic theory model

Arrange marbles in a tray having two wooden partitions glued to it, as shown in Fig. 7.5. Agitate the tray and observe the motion of the marbles (molecules) in the 'solid', 'liquid' and 'gas' compartments.

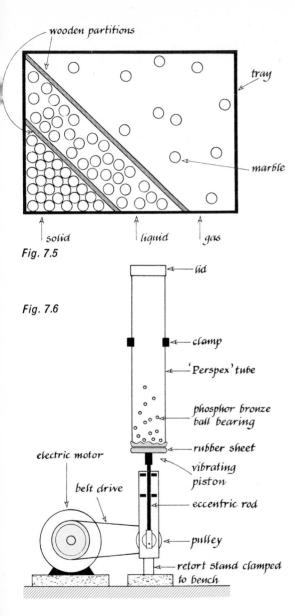

wooden partitions

tray

marble

solid   liquid   gas

Fig. 7.5

Fig. 7.6

lid

clamp

'Perspex' tube

phosphor bronze ball bearing

rubber sheet

vibrating piston

eccentric rod

electric motor

belt drive

pulley

retort stand clamped to bench

Demonstration 7.9. Three-dimensional kinetic theory model of a gas

The model shown in Fig. 7.6 is useful for providing a picture of the behaviour of the molecules of a gas. 'Gas molecules', represented by small phosphor-bronze ball-bearings, are set in motion by a vibrating piston, arranged when in its average position to be 1 or 2 mm below the rubber base of the 'Perspex' tube. There should be enough balls to cover about two-thirds of the base. An electric motor (usually 0–12 volts d.c.) drives the piston up and down via an eccentrically mounted rod. The brass cap on top of the tube reduces noise and prevents the balls escaping.

Gradually increase the voltage applied to the motor until the balls are made to fly up into the tube, dashing hither and thither and having frequent collisions with one another and with the walls of the tube.

A loose-fitting cardboard disk attached to a long wire can be put inside the tube and its weight supported by the upward pressure of the 'gas molecules'.

Finally, if an expanded polystyrene ball (1 cm diameter) is dropped in among the balls its irregular motion illustrates Brownian motion on a large scale.

Q. 7.5 (a) Why are gases more easily squeezed than liquids or solids?

(b) Why is a liquid rather than a gas used to test steel gas-cylinders which have to withstand a high pressure?

Q. 7.6 A liquid does not, like a solid, keep its shape but runs all over the place. What does this suggest about the forces holding the molecules together in a liquid compared with in a solid?

Skin effect in liquids

How small are atoms? Make a rough guess at how many you think could lie side by side along a line 1 cm long. Would it be 1000 (10^3) or 10,000 (10^4) or what? Make a note of your estimate at the back of your notebook. Soon you will measure the size of a molecule and from that the size of an atom can be guessed. To understand what you will be doing, we must study liquid surfaces first.

Experiment 7.10. Investigating liquid surfaces and films

A Gently drop a double-edged razor-blade (*take care*) on to the surface of water in a dish so that it floats. The blade is made of steel which is much denser than water. Why doesn't it sink?
B Dissolve some detergent in a dish of water and make it 'soapy' by stirring with a pencil. Dip

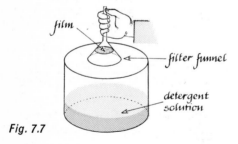

Fig. 7.7

an inverted filter funnel in it so that a film is formed across the wide end. Hold the funnel as in Fig. 7.7 and note what happens.
C Dip a wire frame into the detergent solution and slowly withdraw it collecting a film in the process. Drop a cotton loop on the film, Fig. 7.8, and break the film inside the loop with a pencil.

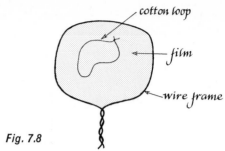

Fig. 7.8

Observe the shape of the loop now. Why does it have this particular shape?

These experiments suggest that the surfaces of liquids (in a vessel or in the form of films) behave like thin elastic skins which are trying to have as small an area as possible. Of course, there is not a real skin on the surface but the liquid acts as if there were.

Why do liquids show the 'skin effect'? The molecules in a liquid attract their neighbours unless they approach very closely, as in a collision, when they repel. A molecule such as *A*, Fig. 7.9, inside the liquid, is on the average attracted equally in all directions. One such as *B*, on the surface, has no liquid molecules above it and most of the attractive forces on it will be downwards. All surface molecules experience this inwards pull which shows up by the surface behaving like an elastic skin, ready to shrink when given the chance.

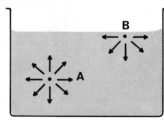

Fig. 7.9

Reducing the skin effect

We will now investigate how adding other substances to a clean liquid surface can alter its skin effect.

Experiment 7.11. Contaminating a water surface

A Thoroughly clean a crystallizing-dish with detergent solution and then rinse it several times with clean water. Fill it to overflowing with water and holding the outside, *with the fingers well away from the rim*, sharply tip out half the water. Lightly sprinkle the water surface with lycopodium powder from a dispenser, Fig. 7.10.

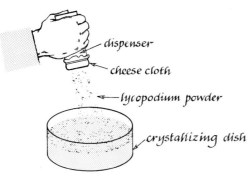

dispenser

cheese cloth

lycopodium powder

crystallizing dish

Fig. 7.10

(Lycopodium is a fine waterproof powder obtained from plants called club-mosses.) Allow a drop of methylated spirit from a dropping-tube to fall on the centre of the powdered surface. Note what happens. (If nothing or very little happens the dish has not been properly cleaned.) *B* Wash out the dish, add fresh water and lycopodium powder and insert the end of a matchstick which has been dipped in olive-oil. Observe the result. In *A* the methylated spirit either dissolved in the water or evaporated. Does olive-oil do this?

C After cleaning the dish with detergent solution and water as before, dip a 'clean' finger in the surface dusted with lycopodium powder. Note the result. Is your finger really clean?

D Thoroughly clean the dish again and fill it with water. Drop a few crumbs of camphor (scraped off a larger piece with a knife) on the water and observe their antics.

How can these results be explained? One explanation would be that on those parts of the surface where something is added to the water, the skin effect is reduced and the surrounding uncontaminated surface, now having a stronger skin, pulls out the added substance (i.e. methylated spirit, olive-oil or grease from your finger) and the powder. The irregular motion of the small pieces of camphor is due to the camphor not dissolving equally at all points and so the skin is weakened more at some places than others.

The cleaning action of detergents depends on their ability to weaken the skin effect of water. Instead of forming drops as it normally does when it meets grease and dirt, the water spreads into all corners and thoroughly wets the dirty article.

Q. 7.7 *Home experiment.* Gently place a small needle on the surface of some water in a dish so that it floats. If you have difficulty, float it on a small piece of blotting-paper and then carefully push the paper below the surface. Add some detergent to the water and explain what happens to the needle.

Q. 7.8 *Home experiment*. Turn an empty jam-jar upside-down and let a drop of water fall on the bottom. How does the drop behave? Dry the bottom and cover an area about the size of a penny with molten wax from a lighted candle. Now allow a drop of water to fall on the solidified wax. What happens this time? Squirt some washing-up liquid (detergent) on the water. Explain what happens.

Oil film experiment

We can now try to find the size of a molecule. Olive-oil will be used because it has an easy molecule to measure. The procedure will be to place a small drop of the oil, of known volume, on a clean water surface, lightly sprinkled with lycopodium powder, in a large tray and then to measure the size of the patch to which it spreads.

A short calculation will give the thickness of the oil patch (film). What does the thickness mean in terms of molecules? If the film spreads out as thinly as it possibly can it will be one molecule thick but if it doesn't it could be . . . . . .? We will be bold and guess that it is one molecule thick and see how our result compares with that obtained from other methods of finding molecular sizes.

Experiment 7.12. Estimating the thickness of an oil film

The tray, previously waxed (see Appendix 6, p. 110), should be arranged, if it is not already, with the drain-hole clear of the bench and the rubber stopper inserted from below. It should be half-filled with clean tap water, levelled using rubber wedges, then filled to *overbrimming* and re-levelled if necessary.

Clean the water surface by slowly drawing the two waxed booms along it, Fig. 7.11, from the

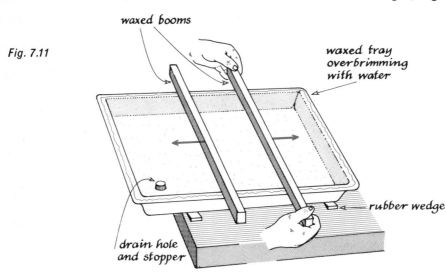

waxed booms

Fig. 7.11

waxed tray overbrimming with water

rubber wedge

drain hole and stopper

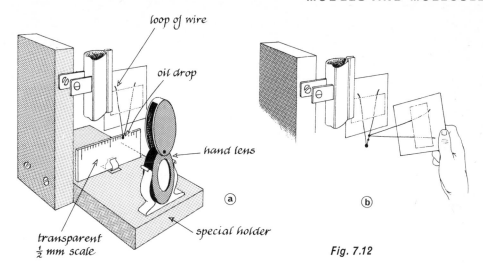

loop of wire

oil drop

hand lens

special holder

transparent
½ mm scale

(a) (b)

Fig. 7.12

middle of the tray to the ends. Leave the booms at the ends.

Insert a transparent scale marked in ½ mm and a hand-lens, in the special holder, Fig. 7.12a, and clamp the holder at eye-level in a retort-stand. Dip the loop of thin steel wire mounted on a card in a small beaker of olive-oil and take up a small drop. Carefully fix the card in the holder so that the drop and the ½ mm scale are seen clearly through the lens. Dip a second wire loop in the oil and use it to help to form a drop, which you judge to be ½ mm in diameter, on the first loop. Small drops can be run together on the first loop as shown in Fig. 7.12b.

Lightly dust the water in the tray with lycopodium powder from the dispenser. Carefully remove the loop with the ½ mm oil drop from the holder and dip its lower end in the water in the *centre* of the tray, Fig. 7.13. Measure the *maximum* diameter of the patch produced with a metre ruler. Clean the surface using the

booms, repeat the experiment with another ½ mm drop and take the average of the two results for the diameter of the patch.

Fig. 7.13

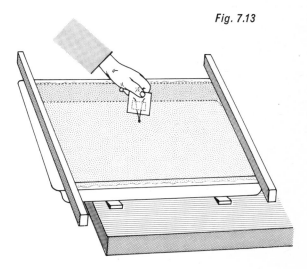

Notes. 1. It may be found that with some tap water the patch contracts soon after forming. A possible cause is water-softening chemicals in the supply attacking the oil but in all cases measure the maximum diameter.

2. It is usually possible for four pupils each to do the experiment twice, before the tray has to be emptied, washed (with the booms) and filled afresh.

3. To empty the tray place a bucket under the drain-hole and remove the rubber stopper. The tray should be washed carefully (to avoid damaging the wax) in a detergent solution and rinsed several times.

Calculating the size of a molecule

How is the thickness of the patch calculated from the volume of the oil drop and the diameter of the patch? The drop is a sphere (a round ball) and the patch circular. However, it makes the arithmetic easier if we assume that:

(*a*) the circular patch is a square with sides of the same length as the diameter of the patch, Fig. 7.14*a* and

(*b*) the drop is a cube whose sides all equal the diameter of the drop, i.e. $\frac{1}{2}$ mm or 1/20 cm, Fig. 7.14*b*.

This may strike you as being a rather unsatisfactory procedure for scientists but it does simplify the calculation and although it does make the result slightly smaller than it should be, we do get an approximate answer. This is better than no answer at all because the calculation otherwise is rather difficult.

We can now proceed, remembering that:

$$Area = length \times breadth$$
$$and, \; Volume = length \times breadth \times height$$
$$\therefore \; Area \; of \; 'square' \; oil \; patch$$
$$= \quad cm \times \quad cm$$
$$= \quad cm^2$$
$$Volume \; of \; 'cubical' \; oil \; drop$$
$$= \frac{1}{20} cm \times \frac{1}{20} cm \times \frac{1}{20} cm$$
$$= \quad cm^3$$

Also, volume of patch = area of patch × thickness of patch.

Now work out the thickness as a fraction of a centimetre.

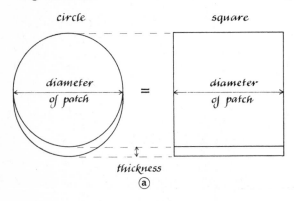

circle   *square*

diameter of patch = diameter of patch

thickness

(a)

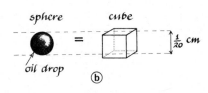

sphere   *cube*

oil drop = $\frac{1}{20}$ cm

(b)

Fig. 7.14

Fig. 7.15a Why can this pond skater walk over the water without sinking?

Fig. 7.15b Water tends to form small drops whenever it can and does so when it falls as rain. What causes this behaviour?

Fig. 7.15c A high-speed photograph of a drop of water that has just left a tap. What keeps the drop together?

We can get an estimate for the size of an atom if we use the information, obtained by chemists, that olive-oil molecules have one end which is attracted strongly to water and the other not. The molecules are therefore upright in the oil patch like bristles in a brush and the thickness of the patch gives the *length* of the olive-oil molecule—assuming it is one molecule thick. We also know from chemical investigations that the length of the olive-oil molecule is taken up by twelve carbon atoms. Dividing the result you got for the thickness of the film by twelve will give the size of one carbon atom.

The accepted value for the diameter of a carbon atom is just over

$$\frac{1}{100,000,000}\,cm = \frac{1}{10^8}\,cm.$$

How does this compare with your answer? Are we justified in assuming that the oil film is one molecule thick?

A word of caution is necessary. Nowadays we no longer picture atoms as having a hard, definite surface like a cricket-ball and so there is no point in trying to give their sizes too exactly.

Q. 7.9 A tray is 50 cm long and 40 cm wide and has 2000 cm³ of water poured into it. What is the depth of water?

Q. 7.10 A drop of an oily liquid of volume $\frac{1}{1000}$ cm³ spreads out on a clean water surface to a film of area 1 m² (i.e. 100×100 cm²). Calculate the thickness of the film.

Q. 7.11 If a certain atom is a sphere and has a diameter of $\frac{1}{10^8}$ cm, how many could lie side by side along a line 1 cm long? Compare your answer with the estimate you wrote down at the back of your notebook before you did the oil film experiment.

Q. 7.12 There are tiny holes in the rubber of a balloon through which a gas can escape. In the exhibition of materials at the beginning of the course you may have noticed that the balloon containing hydrogen went down after a day whilst those containing air and carbon dioxide stayed up much longer. What can you say about the size of these gas molecules?

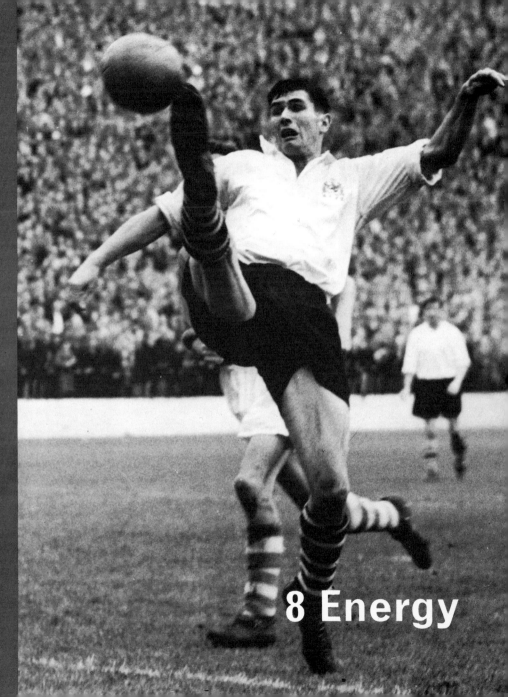

Energy—where
does it come from?
A Bristol City
footballer in action

8 Energy

CHAPTER EIGHT ENERGY

Jobs, food and fuel

Jobs have to be done by all of us at home, at school and at play. To be energetic, like the footballer on p. 97, and do jobs we require a regular and plentiful supply of food. Do all jobs have to be 'food-using?' If you stand holding a pile of books you become tired but the same job could be done by a table and no 'feeding' of the table would be necessary.

Experiment 8.1. Doing 'jobs'

Do these simple jobs and discuss whether they need food.
A Blow up a balloon.
B Sit and look at the blown-up balloon lying on the bench.
C Hold a rubber band between your hands, stretch it and then let go.
D Raise a block of wood or a brick or some other object from the floor to the bench by pulling on a string tied to the object.
E Place a book as a paper-weight on top of some loose papers.
F Fix a pulley to the edge of the bench, run a string, tied to an object on the floor, over the pulley and raise the object by pulling the string along the bench, Fig. 8.1.

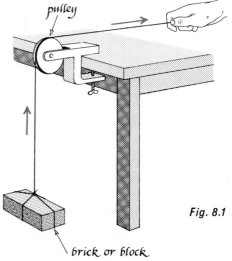

pulley

brick or block

Fig. 8.1

98

Nowadays jobs can often be done by machines, some of these also need to be 'fed'. A machine like a motor-car has an engine which has to be supplied with petrol; others, such as a washing-machine, have an electric motor that requires 'feeding' from the electricity supply. Petrol is a fuel as are coal, wood, gas, coke and diesel oil.

Many jobs require food and fuels and it is in these that scientists and engineers are often most interested.

Q. 8.1 Which of these jobs use food or fuel?
(*a*) Hitting a cricket-ball with a bat or a tennis-ball with a racket.
(*b*) A concrete post holding up a fence.
(*c*) Climbing a hill.
(*d*) Learning history.
(*e*) A bulldozer clearing a building site.
(*f*) A self-winding watch winding itself up.
(*g*) A vacuum cleaner picking up dust.
(*h*) Water keeping someone afloat in a swimming-pool.
(*i*) A helicopter hovering at a constant height above a ship in distress.

Energy and some of its forms

Scientists consider that food and fuels are stores of something called *energy* and that it is energy which enables men and machines to do useful jobs. One of the important things about energy is that there are many kinds or forms of it.

1. CHEMICAL ENERGY

The food you eat supplies chemicals to your muscles and when you raise a load or push something along your muscles use some of these chemicals, so producing energy which enables

you to do the job. In fact food is just as much a fuel for the human machine as petrol is fuel for a car and coal is fuel for a power station. The energy obtained from the chemicals in food and fuels is called *chemical energy*.

2. UPHILL ENERGY

Demonstration 8.2. Using a falling brick to raise a weight

Lift a brick from the floor to bench-level, tie a length of string to it and allow it to raise a 1 kg load using a pulley as in Fig. 8.2.

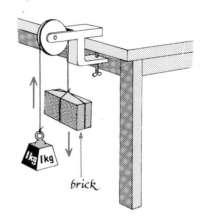

Fig. 8.2

The brick in falling does a useful job by raising the load and must therefore have had energy at bench-level. We will call the energy of a raised object *uphill energy*. Notice that to raise the brick and give it uphill energy your muscles had to use some chemical energy. This is another important thing about energy, one form can be changed into another.

3. MOTION ENERGY

Demonstration 8.3. Using a falling brick to break a board

Lift a brick from the floor and allow it to fall from bench-level and break a piece of hardboard, Fig. 8.3.

Fig. 8.3

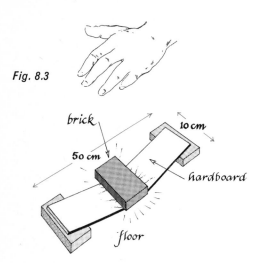

The brick had uphill energy at bench-level but just before it reached the hardboard this had been used up. A useful job was done by the brick as it came to rest at the bottom of its fall and so it must have had some kind of energy just before it hit the board. We consider that it had energy because of the motion it gained by falling. We will call the energy of a moving body *motion energy*. In this case chemical energy in your muscles was changed to uphill energy of the brick when you raised it and then the uphill energy changed to motion energy as the brick fell.

In Fig. 8.4 a building is being demolished by a 'drop ball' which is slowly raised by the crane and then suddenly dropped. What changes occur in the forms of energy during the operation?

Fig. 8.4

4. SPRINGS ENERGY

Demonstration 8.4. Raising a weight by a spring

Keep a spring stretched whilst you attach a small load to the lower end as in Fig. 8.5. Release the spring and the load rises.

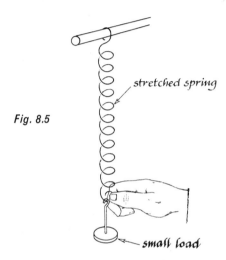

stretched spring

Fig. 8.5

small load

A useful job has been done by the stretched spring; it is said to have *springs energy*.

5. ELECTRICAL ENERGY

Electric trains connected to an electricity supply can do jobs such as moving people and goods from one place to another. The energy we get from the electricity supply is called *electrical energy*. At many power stations in Britain the chemical energy in coal is changed to electrical energy.

There are other kinds of energy which you will learn about later; for the present we will consider only one more—atomic energy.

Q. 8.2 In the following jobs say how the forms of energy change.

(*a*) A builder uses a pulley to raise a bucket of mortar from the ground to a higher level, Fig. 8.6.

pulley

Fig. 8.6

(b) A pile-driver working from a Diesel engine drives a steel pile (tube) into soft ground to make a firm foundation for a building, Fig. 8.7.

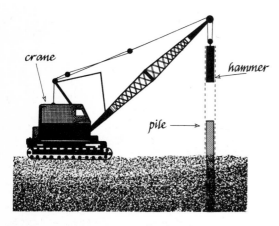

Fig. 8.7

Fig. 8.8

Fig. 8.9

(c) A boy fires a paper pellet using a stretched rubber band as a catapult.

(d) An electric motor raises the lift in a department store from the basement to the top floor.

(e) The mainspring of a watch is wound up.

Atomic energy

Atoms themselves have a store of energy and in a few cases it has been possible to release this energy and harness it to do useful jobs. Uranium, the heaviest of the naturally occurring elements, provides atomic energy when its atoms are broken up. It is mined in places such as South Africa, Fig. 8.8, but it must be purified and made into rods before it is used. Fig. 8.9 shows the

rods being transported in cases and in Fig. 8.10 you can see the rods loaded in the machine which lowers them into the 'reactor' where the atomic energy is released.

In an atomic power station the energy produces electricity. Britain's first atomic power station, built at Calder Hall in Cumberland, opened in 1956, Fig. 8.11. In an atomic submarine the energy propels the submarine. The first atomic submarine, *Nautilus*, Fig. 8.12, was built by the Americans and during a trip of 80,000 kilometres it used only about 4 kg of uranium. The same journey in a normal submarine would have required 8 million kilogrammes of oil.

Whereas energy is set free gradually in an 'atomic reactor', in an 'atomic bomb' it is released all at once and produces a tremendous explosion accompanied by dangerous radiation. When the first bomb was tested in 1945 in the desert of New Mexico, U.S.A., the heat was so intense that the desert sand near the explosion became molten glass.

Fig. 8.10

Fig. 8.11
Calder Hall
nuclear power station

A Cooling towers
B Cooling towers
C Nuclear reactors
D Sub-station
E Turbine hall
F Heat exchanger

Fig. 8.12
Nautilus at
Portsmouth

Radioactive atoms

The atoms of some of the heavier elements such as radium break up of their own accord and shoot out high-speed particles. These particles have, for their size, large amounts of energy (motion energy) obtained from the energy store of the exploding atom. Atoms that behave in this way are said to be *radioactive*.

Using a cloud chamber it is possible to see the tracks followed by the ejected, high-speed particles, although the particles themselves are much too small to be seen. There are two kinds of cloud chamber and before we use the first, called the expansion cloud chamber, a demonstration will help to explain how it works.

Demonstration 8.5. Cloud formation

A Pour a little water into an empty Winchester bottle. Pump some air into it from a bicycle pump (about 12 strokes), Fig. 8.13, then remove the rubber stopper so that the air expands rapidly. View the bottle against a dark background.

B Repeat the whole process several times and see what happens each time.

C Put a lighted match into the bottle, pump in air and remove the stopper. What is the difference?

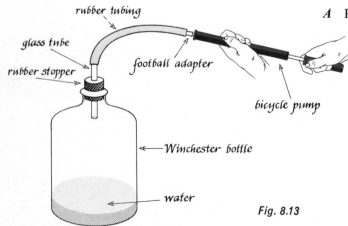

rubber tubing

glass tube

rubber stopper

football adapter

bicycle pump

Winchester bottle

water

Fig. 8.13

The previous demonstration shows that clouds can be made by allowing air containing water vapour to expand rapidly and that when smoke or dust is present a thicker cloud forms. The smoke and dust act as centres on which the water drops making up the cloud can form. In the expansion cloud chamber the particles shot out by the radioactive atoms cause damage in the air through which they pass and leave 'things' (you will learn about these later) that help water drops to start, as smoke and dust do, when there is an expansion.

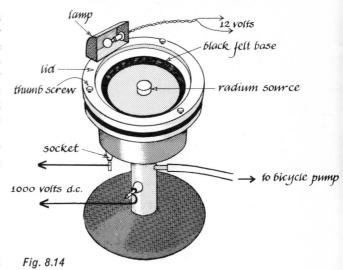

Fig. 8.14

Cloud chambers

Both types of chamber show the tracks due to particles, called *alpha particles*, which are shot out from exploding radium atoms.

Demonstration 8.6. Expansion cloud chamber

The setting-up instructions depend on the make of the cloud chamber and are usually supplied with the instrument. In the one shown in Fig. 8.14 the lid and glass are first removed by undoing the three thumb screws and then the black felt base moistened with methylated spirit. Before replacing the glass, rubber ring and lid, moisten the faces of the lower rubber ring with methylated spirit to obtain a good seal. Tighten the thumb screws evenly and arrange the lamp so that it will shine away from you.

Connect the chamber by the two sockets provided to a power supply (E.H.T.) of about 1000 volts and connect the lamp to a 12 volt supply. Attach the bicycle pump supplied to the inlet on the apparatus by rubber tubing.

Expansion of the air in the chamber is achieved by withdrawing, fairly rapidly, the piston of the pump and holding it withdrawn. (The leather cup washer in the pump is reversed and so air is removed from the chamber.) Once the initial mist has cleared after the first few strokes, long straight tracks similar to those in Fig. 8.15

Fig. 8.15

should be seen coming from the very weak radium source secured to the centre of the base. About 5 seconds should be allowed between expansions.

If the tracks are spoilt at any point by a streaming effect from the edge of the chamber, either tighten the lid using the appropriate thumb screw or remove the lid and moisten the rubber ring with methylated spirit.

You will understand better how the diffusion cloud chamber works when you have done more physics but it is an improvement on the expansion type because it works continuously.

Experiment 8.7. Diffusion cloud chamber

Set up the chamber, Fig. 8.16, by removing the lid and moistening the felt ring round the inside of the top with methylated spirit from a dropping-tube.

Invert the chamber, unscrew the base and remove the foam plastic cushion. Cover the lower surface of the floor with small pieces of solid carbon dioxide (use gloves) or with carbon dioxide snow, to a depth of a few millimetres. Replace the cushion and screw on the base. Set the chamber upright, replace the 'Perspex' lid and level with the three rubber wedges.

Direct a beam of light horizontally through the chamber just above the cork ring. Rub the lid with a handkerchief and in less than a minute tracks should be seen coming from the radium source in the small cup at the end of the crank-shaped wire.

Notes. 1. Adjust the levelling of the chamber if the tracks drift rapidly in one direction.

2. Rub the lid frequently to keep the tracks sharp.

3. The chamber will go on working so long as there is methylated spirit in the felt ring and solid carbon dioxide in the base.

4. See Appendix 4, concerning supplies of solid carbon dioxide ('dry ice').

What happens in a cloud chamber is rather like what would occur in a ripe cornfield through

Fig. 8.16

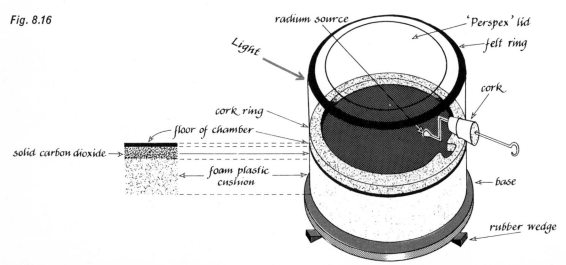

which a cannon-ball is fired. If you were watching from above in a helicopter, you would certainly not see the ball and you would not notice the track of broken stalks until some time after when it would be marked by a line of blackbirds feeding on the fallen heads.

Q. 8.3 Mr Y. Howe has been examining the cloud chamber tracks in Fig. 8.15 and says there are one or two interesting things to be seen. Can you notice any of them?

Spark counter

Alpha particles from a radioactive substance can also be detected by a spark counter. You will learn later how this works but for the present it is interesting to see it in action.

Demonstration 8.8. Spark counter

The counter consists of a strip of wire gauze joined by a metal plate to a black terminal and a narrow metal strip just below the gauze which is connected to a red terminal, Fig. 8.17. Join the red terminal to the positive of an E.H.T. supply (without any 50 MΩ safety resistor) and the black terminal to E.H.T.— and earth, as shown.

Increase the voltage until sparking just occurs when it should be reduced *very slightly* until sparking *just* stops. Usually about 4500 volts is required.

If a radium source is held 1 or 2 cm above the gauze, sparks should be seen and heard when alpha particles are present in the space between the gauze and the narrow metal strip. Do the sparks occur at regular intervals?

If pieces of paper and aluminium leaf are placed in turn between the source and the gauze,

the penetrating power of alpha particles can be investigated.

The range of the alpha particles in air may also be found roughly by gradually raising the source until sparking just stops.

Q. 8.4 *Home experiment.* You can do this at home if you have a watch with a luminous dial. Take your watch and a hand-lens into a really dark cupboard or room and wait for 5 minutes until your eyes have become accustomed to the dark. Then examine the luminous figures carefully with the hand-lens. You should see something interesting.

The paint on the hands and figures of the watch contains a very small amount of a radioactive substance mixed with luminous material (like that on the screen of a television tube) which gives out a flash of light when it is struck by an alpha particle. Would it be true to say that you are seeing atoms explode before your eyes?

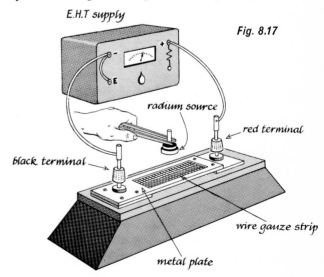

Fig. 8.17

APPENDIXES

Appendix 1. Suggested materials for Exhibition

So far as possible materials which are common in the home should be used. Some may have to be labelled and bottles should be left open unless there is potential danger. Where materials cannot be left out on display it may be necessary to pass them round the class but there should be an opportunity for handling, weighing, smelling, etc.

Alum (crystal)
Aluminium (block)
Balloon of air
Balloon of carbon dioxide
Balloon of coal-gas (or hydrogen)
Bleach
Bottle labelled 'air'
Bottle labelled 'vacuum'
Brass (block)
Brick
Calcite (crystal)
Car oil
Cellulose acetate
Ceramic
Chalk
Coal
Coke
Common salt
Copper sulphate (crystal)
Copper wire
Cotton fabric
Expanded polystyrene
Fat

Flour
Gelatine
Glass (block)
Granite
Hardwood
Iron (block)
Jelly
Latex foam
Lead (block)
Limestone
Marble (block)
Mercury
Mica
Nylon fabric
Olive-oil
Paraffin wax
'Perspex'
Polythene
Quartz
Rayon fabric
Rubber
Sandstone
Silk fabric
Slate
Soap

Softwood
Steel spring
Sugar
Sulphur (flowers)

Vinegar
Washing soda
Woollen fabric

Some of the above can be obtained from the Nuffield materials, crystals and elastic materials kits.

Large balloons, filled just before display, should be used. If cylinders of hydrogen and carbon dioxide are available they can be used if the regulator valve is carefully controlled.

Appendix 2. Rotary vacuum pumps

Brief operating instructions for two makes of pump are given.

(a) NGN Forevac pump unit, Fig. A2.1.

Connect the vessel to be evacuated to the *inlet* tube of the *butterfly valve* using pressure tubing. Check that the butterfly valve is open (i.e. lever arm vertical) and switch on the pump motor.

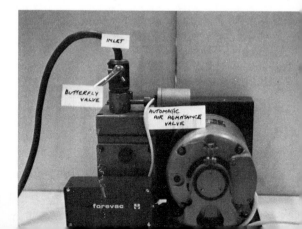

Fig. A2.1

After evacuating, close the butterfly valve (i.e lever arm horizontal) and switch off the pump.

To release the vacuum, open the butterfly valve thus allowing air to enter by the *automatic air admittance valve*.

(b) Edward's 'Speedivac' pump

If the arrangement shown in Fig. A2.2 is used, connect whatever is to be evacuated to the pump *inlet* tube (below the Bourdon pressure gauge) by pressure tubing. Check that the *diaphragm valve* below the baseplate is open and that the *air admittance valve* is closed (i.e. knob turned fully clockwise). Also block the hole in the centre of the baseplate with a rubber bung or cap. Switch on the pump motor.

After evacuating, close the diaphragm valve tightly and switch off the pump. To release the vacuum allow air to enter by opening the air admittance valve (i.e. turn knob anti-clockwise till hissing is heard).

Notes.

1. It is important that the procedure given in the previous paragraph is followed, otherwise pump oil may be forced back into the vessel evacuated.

2. When it is desired to evacuate slowly, the air admittance valve can be opened as far as is required to give the appropriate rate.

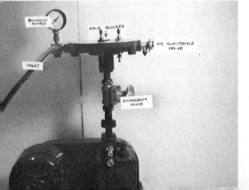

Fig. A2.2

Appendix 3. The 'black-box' experiment

Small coffee- or syrup-tins painted black, sealed and bound with tape can be used as the 'black-boxes'. Suitable objects include a golf ball, a metal cube, a metal cylinder, a large rubber stopper, a small lemon.

Appendix 4. Supplies of solid carbon dioxide

Supplies of solid carbon dioxide ('dry ice') can be obtained in two ways.

(*a*) *Blocks of 'dry ice'.* These are sold as 'Drikold' by I.C.I. and as 'Cardice' by D.C.L. Addresses of local depots from which supplies are available may be obtained by writing either to:

Imperial Chemical Industries Ltd
London Sales Office
Templar House
P.O. Box 19
81–87 High Holborn
London W.C.1

or to:

Distillers Co. Ltd
Carbon Dioxide Division
Cedar House
39 London Road
Reigate, Surrey

It is also sometimes possible to obtain small amounts from a local ice-cream manufacturer, a meat wholesaler, a sausage factory, the waterworks or a local university.

'*Dry ice*' *should never be handled without gloves*. It can be stored in a 'Thermos' flask with a loose plug of paper or cotton-wool for 36–48 hours. It is readily broken into small pieces if it is wrapped in a cloth and struck with a hammer.

(*b*) *Cylinders of liquid carbon dioxide*. Small quantities of 'dry ice' can be made using an attachment which is fitted on a cylinder of liquid carbon dioxide.

Cylinders are of two types—siphon and standard; the latter has to be inverted when used. In both cases the valve on the cylinder is opened *fully* to allow about a 5-second burst of carbon dioxide to expand out of the nozzle on the attachment into a closely woven cloth (supplied with the attachment) and a 250 cm^3 beaker, as shown in Fig. A4.1. Immediately after the expansion any carbon dioxide 'snow' adhering to the inside of the cloth can be scraped into the beaker.

D.C.L. operate a cylinder refilling service, and addresses of local depots can be obtained from the above address. If a local service is not available contact may be made with:

The Speedy CO$_2$ Service Co.
16 Clement Street, Birmingham 1.

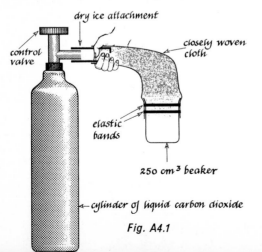

dry ice attachment

control valve

closely woven cloth

elastic bands

250 cm^3 beaker

cylinder of liquid carbon dioxide

Fig. A4.1

Appendix 5. Preparation of expendable steel springs

These springs are supplied as Nuffield item 2A. Two points may require attention before use.

(*a*) If the coils are touching they should be separated by *gently loading* the spring with about 500 g.

(*b*) Some springs are supplied with the loops at the ends already soldered to prevent them coming undone when loads are attached. When loops have to be soldered they should be cleaned with emery paper, dipped first in flux (killed spirits) and then in a tin lid of molten solder.

Appendix 6. Waxing of trays and booms for the oil film experiment

(*a*) Waterproofing the trays and booms with wax enables a clean water surface to be obtained readily. It should be done at least one day before they are to be used.

To wax one tray heat $\frac{1}{4}$ kg of new paraffin wax in a can until the hot liquid *just starts* to smoke. Stir in a little vegetable black, this ensures that the patch of oil will be easily visible against the background of the tray. Quickly paint the tray and booms using a soft paintbrush (5 cm wide). *Only the rim of the tray needs to have a smooth wax surface*. Any roughness will be due to the molten wax not being hot enough and can usually be removed by repainting with very hot wax.

(*b*) It is recommended that if possible the trays are set out, filled to overbrimming with water, ready for use before the lesson.

(*c*) The trays should be stored between corrugated paper to prevent damage to the wax but chipped parts can be repainted.

Appendix 7. List of Nuffield apparatus used in Book One

Nuffield number	*Item*
1	Materials kit
2	Elastic materials kit
3	Crystals kit
4	Microbalance kit
5	Lever kit
6	Bristol pressure kit
7	Oil film kit
10	Year 1 general kit
11	Kinetic theory model kit
12	Two-dimensional kinetic model kit
13	Vacuum pump
14	E.H.T. power supply
16	Radium source
17	Spark counter
18	Expansion cloud chamber
19/1	Carbon dioxide cylinder
19/2	Dry ice attachment for above
22	Atom model
23	Microscopes (8)
24	Hand lenses (32)
25	Plastic measuring rules (32)
26	'Perspex' containers (16)
27	Transformers (0—12 V, 6 A) (8)
28	Diffusion cloud chambers (8)
29	Whitley Bay smoke cells (8)
30	Slotted bases (16)
31/1	Weight hangers with slotted 10 g weights (16)
31/2	Weight hangers with slotted 100 g weights (16)
32	Weights 1 kg (16)
33	Paper scales (32)
40	Single pulleys on clamp (2)
41	Evesham pressure apparatus
42	Lever-arm balances (8)
45	Foot pump and adapter
47	Lamps (8)
50/1	Pairs of cylindrical magnets (32)
67	Bourdon gauge
150	Laboratory motor, 12 volts d.c.
523	Aspirator (10 litre)
528	Crystallizing dishes (16)
543	Chinagraph pencils (4)

A complete kit contains apparatus for 32 pupils working singly, in pairs or in fours. The Year 1 general kit contains many useful items which are not always easily obtainable. Export economy kits are also available.

Appendix 8. Visual aids

Chapter 1. Matter

16 mm films	*Rocks that form on the earth's surface*[1]
	Rocks that originate underground[1]
	The birth and death of mountains[2]

Chapter 2. Crystals

16 mm film	*Crystals* (P.S.S.C.)[3]

Chapter 3. Measuring

16 mm films	*Measuring large distances* (P.S.S.C.)[3]
	Measuring short distances (P.S.S.C.)[3]
	Time and clocks (P.S.S.C.)[3]
Filmstrips	*Mapping the earth's surface*[4]
	The story of time[4]
	Time and direction[4]

Chapter 6. Pressure

Filmstrip | *The earth's atmosphere* [4]
Chart | *The earth's atmosphere* [4]

Chapter 7. Models and molecules

16 mm films | *Evidence for molecules and atoms* [1]
| *Behaviour of gases* (P.S.S.C.) [3]
Filmstrip | *The structure of matter* [5]

Chapter 8. Energy

Filmstrip | *Energy and man, Parts* 1, 2, 5 [6]
Chart | *Energy—key to all activity* [7]

Film for teachers

An approach to kinetic theory [7]

Addresses

1. Rank Film Library, 1 Aintree Road, Perivale, Greenford, Middlesex.

2. Boulton-Hawker Films, Hadleigh, Suffolk.

3. Sound-Services Film Library, Wilton Crescent, Merton Park, London S.W.19.

4. Educational Productions Ltd, East Ardsley, Wakefield, Yorkshire.

5. Common Ground Ltd, 44 Fulham Road, London S.W.3.

6. Visual Publications Ltd, 197 Kensington High Street, London W.8.

7. Esso Film Library, c/o Travelling Films, 60/66 Wardour Street, London W.1.

INDEX